Our most important
task each and every day
is to remember we exist.

Published independently by Sebastian Kade

Learn more at www.sebastiankade.com

First Published 2017

Sebastian Kade asserts the moral right to be identified
as the author of this work

© Sebastian Kade 2017

Set in 10.3/14.214 pt Palatino
Typeset by Sebastian Kade (AUS), Sydney

Every reasonable effort has been made to seek the
permission of the copyright holders and publishers whose
work as been quoted herein. The publishers would be
interested to hear from any copyright
holders who have not been acknowledged.

LIVING HAPPINESS

A PERSONAL MANIFESTO FOR LIVING

Dedicated to myself.

To love oneself wholly and truly is the key to life; only when it interferes with our ability to love others should we call it vanity.

eh...

Dedicated to my *self,* family and friends.

Contents

Author Foreword

Before I can start a book on happiness, I have to answer the looming question that nearly every reader will have: "Who are you to write a book on happiness? And why should I trust you?"

To be frank, you shouldn't. This book is written in such a way that at every step, the logic and reasoning is plainly laid out to be thoroughly questioned and tested by yourself. Or, as the wise Buddha put it thousands of years ago, *"Examine my words as a goldsmith tests gold, by burning, cutting and rubbing. Only then should these words be accepted."*

To be more elaborate, this book isn't really written by me. It is written by the thousands of great thinkers that have come before me. Thinkers dating back thousands of years who spent their lives pondering the human existence and putting their learnings to paper.

While my personal story is irrelevant to the ideas put forth in this book, I believe a brief background of myself will add richness to the voice with which you read it.

I had an extremely fortunate upbringing in a loving household. My parents' constant drive for betterment was ingrained in me as a child. Driving to weekend sport was accompanied by audio tapes of Tony Robbins. You could say that self improvement was the soundtrack of my childhood. This foundation jump-started my career, enabling me to reach corporate "success" early on. I think it is natural for many of us to search for happiness in success. We think that if we get that promotion, if we lead that team, we will be happy. I worked hard, smart and long, eventually reaping the rewards. I had a nice apartment, nice clothes, a new car, travelled around the world, but regardless of all this I wasn't satisfied. I still felt an emptiness that pervaded much of my life. When I was young, I dreamed about the future and how fulfilling it would be. I imagined the "end goal" was a life of satisfaction and happiness. However, after growing up and getting a taste for success I found things to be very different from how I had imagined them. The same expectancy for the future persisted long after my youth had passed away. Eventually it clicked that things might not change. Emptiness became my status quo. I tried to fill it with *things*–purchases, possessions and experiences–but unfortunately the emptiness had an insatiable appetite that devoured anything I sent at it. So I continued buying things and experiences to satisfy the pangs of spiritual hunger.

Looking back on life it is easy to say that I had been looking for happiness for many years, but in the moment it wasn't so clear. In all honesty, it was really just a scramble in the dark, relentlessly searching for something, but for what? I did not know.

This tale of material dissatisfaction is probably nothing new. The emptiness grows into dissatisfaction then into sadness, which either engulfs your mind or you find something else to suppress the inner gnawing. In my case it was building a company. I threw myself into building a successful startup with some smart people and worked unhealthy hours for unhealthy periods of time. I sacrificed luxuries for the hope of being successful again. However this time, the success I pursued took a different form. Startup life is less flashy, but in the end, it is still the pursuit of success. It is easy to throw yourself into work ignoring life, and thanks to our capitalist society, it is both rewarded and respected.

One day I got sick, nothing bad, just a fever that put me off work for a week. Sitting in bed I began to see that I wasn't actually living. My "life" was being spent working towards the lure of success in the hopes of making it big. I was working for a *chance* to start living. That being said, realizations as clear as this only happen in fiction, in the moment they are never so clear.

More honestly, what this realization looked like was a new found feeling of duty to read the "classics" (classic fiction). My first pick was *The Count of Monte Cristo*—arguably one of the greatest books of all time—which got me hooked.

The more classics I read, the more I learnt what made them timeless: story + idea. Every great novel does more than tell a story. It captures a slice of the human experience better than ever before; it contains the essence of what it means to suffer, to love, to live, to be human.

Reading my way through the classics, I began to understand the core thread that ran through them all; the story of human suffering and the search to end it.

Since classic fiction is essentially a form of philosophy, it was no surprise for me to segue into ancient philosophy, namely Stoicism and Buddhism. These two philosophies are, in my opinion, the foundations of all others. They are the birthplace of modern thought and spirituality as we know it.

My journey through classic fiction turned into a year-long voracious appetite for these novels. Churning through book after book, piecing together the gigantic jigsaw puzzle of life.

After a year of reading, thinking and practicing, I couldn't open a new book without seeing the same core ideas written on every page. Like all writers before me, I felt that there was a book missing that had not yet been written, one that looked at happiness through the lens of rationality and logic to build a secular framework for a life of happiness.

This book was written because there are two types of "self-help" books, those on *happiness* and those on *success*. The former discusses ideas on how to conquer your inner-world, the latter on how to conquer the outer-world. There have been countless books written on the success that use logic and rationality to create a framework for becoming "successful". Unfortunately it seems that when it comes to happiness, we throw away the scientific lens in place of the mystical; replace daily habits with daily prayers. Not enough books look at happiness with the same rationale and logic that is used when looking at success. I think it is this distaste for "mystical happiness" that makes many secular people choose success over happiness. However, these two paths are not exclusive, we don't have to choose happiness or success. Instead, we need to review our perception of the two. Success is not happiness, happiness is not success. We can not use the principles of success to achieve happiness, nor can we use the principles of happiness and expect success. It should be of little surprise then if we focus all our time and energy on success and find at the end of the road we have a handful of gold but an empty heart.

In addition, I would by lying if I didn't say that I wrote this book for myself. The framework that is presented here is my personal manifesto for living. It is my attempt to build a scaffold for my life that can guide my thoughts and actions on a day-to-day basis. Putting these words to paper is my way of eternalizing them; by writing this book I have written them in time itself.

So without further adieu, en garde!

Part I

Understanding Happiness

We are thrust into life, tumbled around in our youth, only to come to the surface in time and realize we are living without meaning. This was best put by the French 1940s philosopher Jean-Paul Sartre who coined the phrase "being precedes essence"; meaning that first we exist as human beings and then we find meaning for our existence. Without looking to polarize ourselves on this topic, we can all agree that regardless of whether this definition is true–or if there is a predisposed meaning for us through religion–it is our duty as rational beings to discover it. Whatever we end up deciding our purpose in life is, what we have found is something that brings our state of being into balance; we have found peace with our own existence. This peace we search for is Happiness.

This book itself cannot promise you a happy life; no amount of knowledge can do that. What this book can provide is a journey of exploration through the foundations of happiness. It will build a blueprint for living crafted from the bricks of logic and rationality. We will construct an outlook on life that can be lived each and every day; not just by a few, but by everyone. In other words we will aim to define the lowest common denominator of happiness; one that is applicable, regardless of religious outlook, social status, or level of education.

Most important is remembering that the knowledge we

uncover in this book is of little value until it is practiced in everyday life. As we will see, happiness is not achieved, it is practiced. Hence, the only person who can promise a life of happiness is you.

In essence, this book is a journey of knowledge with the sole purpose being daily enlightenment; clearly seeing life, and yourself, as they truly are. Only then, can we find a clear and steady path to living a life of happiness.

What is Happiness?

There is no happiness in youth, only ignorance; this is where all of man starts off, unaware of a perpetual state of happiness and unaware of the need to search for it.

That is not to say that some youth are not more joyful and some more melancholy, some more sombre and others more passionate. However, all of these are fluctuations in the young mind reacting to the world around it. As the pig is happy in the mud, we would never choose to switch with the pig because the pig is ignorant of its self and situation; likewise the youth.

Without us realizing it, up until this point we have been living under the impression that things make us happy. Since infants we have been getting rewards for doing right, those rewards made us happy. Ergo, we get ice-cream, we are happy. As we grow, this idea that things make us happy sticks with us. Some live their whole lives like this. The things just get bigger and more expensive: we get new phone, we are happy; we get new clothes, we are happy; we get car, we are happy. Although this sounds naive and childish, we often settle into this way of living without consciously choosing it; we inherit this mindset rather than forming it. This is partly due to our capitalistic society, where the idea of material happiness is constantly being reinforced by the media and advertising. It is no surprise then to find that many of us grow up pursuing this false notion of happiness. We often go to extreme measures to further our material possessions, even at the cost of others' well-being. This may sound like an exaggeration on paper, but in reality many of us would be happy to take a pay rise even if came at the cost of another person's job. We are understandably more focused on progressing up the social ladder of "success" than finding true happiness.

Happiness is having things of beauty

In this definition–and in this entire book–the word "beauty" is used in its most general sense, as the recognition of that which is "good". When we say something is beautiful, we are saying that we find it to represent our ideals of goodness in one way or another. A car could be beautiful, not only if it is aesthetically pleasing, but if it reflects what it means to be a good car.

As we acquire more possessions we get accustomed to having more. This then means we need even more to sustain our constant level of happiness. Our desire for things to make us happy leads to an insatiable appetite, turning happiness into a distant, unreachable state. We don't have to go far down this route of material conquest to realize the impossibility of this route.

This all sounds trivial and obvious from the outside, but when stuck in this state of mind all we feel is an inexplicable numbness that lives somewhere out of sight. We feel as though we are endlessly trying to reach our happiness, but in spite of our best efforts we make no traction.

Inevitably, it all comes crashing down, often through a traumatic life event, or simply when we first notice the unbroken monotony of life laying out before us. Realising the emptiness of material happiness leaves us searching for a better definition to live by. By reflecting on the happy times in life, we can see that it has always been in special moments that we find happiness. Holidays. Loves. Triumphs. It was not the things that we owned in these moments that brought us happiness but the moment itself. That road trip we took after graduating. That time we went travelling with our best friend. All these memories bring us bursts of joy and happiness. Our concept of happiness moves from *things* to *moments*.

If we now believe that happiness is found in moments, we can deduct that the path to happiness is to live for the moment.

Happiness is found in
moments of beauty

When examining the people around us, this seems to be the truth. Everyone we know is focused on finding as many happy moments as possible. It is what we spend our money on, how we spend our time.

When happiness is found in certain moments, then the time in between—the filler—is simply there to connect one moment of happiness to another. There are also moments of unhappiness, and hence, the obvious goal is to try to minimize these. In essence, maximise pleasure moments, minimize pain moments, and skip through the filler. The problem with this approach is that this filler gets harder and harder to bear. We begin craving these happy moments and become more and more dependent on finding them. When we do find them, we have desired them for so long that they have no hope of ever living up to our expectations. Or we become sad that the moment has to end, and begin dreaming of the next moment to come.

Today's social media addicted world takes this idea even further. We have become more focused on sharing moments than enjoying them. Constantly looking into each others lives through rose-tinted glasses, assuming that our friends' lives are as happy as their well-crafted timeline appears. We stop finding happiness in the moment as we are too busy capturing it in hopes of gaining social rapport by sharing it.

This manifests in many shapes and forms. Just recently when travelling I caught myself squeezing through the crowd to get a perfect, unobstructed view of some statue, only to snap a picture and move on. Not stopping to actually admire the work that went into carving this sculpture, not stopping to feel the essence of the building, but simply capturing it to share and say, "I've been there". Ironically, this need to share our lives with the world disconnects us from the actual life that we are living. We are missing out on all the opportunities that our friends think we are having; each of us desiring the moments that the other didn't actually have.

Going down this path eventually leads us to a moment of filler that we were unable to fill. Suddenly, you realize how empty your happiness is. Life becomes overwhelmingly filled with lull moments and you are consumed with a constant desire for happy moments. The same insatiable desire that was felt for our possessions, now grows for moments. What seemed like an assured path to happiness, turns out to be no different from our original attempt. Moments, like possessions, can only bring temporary happiness. Over time our brains become adapted to these pleasures to the point that in order to maintain a constant level of happiness we require them to be more frequent and with greater intensity.

Having ruled out material and experiential happiness, what's left? There is a story that can help us find the next step.

In an ancient kingdom there were two Princes. These princes were twins born at exactly the same time, raised exactly the same way. Both twins were loved equally by the King and Queen, however, early in childhood one prince developed a pessimistic outlook on the world—identifying everything that was wrong with it, always finding problems, whereas the other prince had developed the opposite—an optimistic outlook on the world, finding goodness and beauty in everything he saw. When each Prince was given a golden apple, the first Prince complained that it hurt his teeth, while the second admired its weight and shine. Over time, the first Prince grew up to be a miserable man full of jealousy and hatred. He envied his brother's status, wife and fortune. His brother, who later became King, lived a happy life full of joy and gratefulness. One day the sad, angry Prince asked his brother, "Why have you been so lucky to live a happy life while I am cursed to misery?" To which his brother replied "Because I saw it so."

What this simple story highlights is how little our actual environment affects our life. We generally feel as though we could be happier if we had another person's life, yet that person thinks exactly the same about someone else. We often miss the fact that our outlook on a situation has much greater influence over our level of happiness than the situation itself. It was by *finding* beauty in each moment that the happy Prince became so.

What this story suggests is that happiness is the feeling of appreciation; we feel happy when we appreciate beauty in the world around us. When you are surrounded by things, people and moments that you think are beautiful, you feel a sense of happiness. This is accurate in explaining both material and experiential happiness. It even explains the sensualist who finds beauty in his pleasures, and hence, for a brief moment before the insatiable desires kick back in, finds happiness.

What is equally important is the fact that we can consciously find beauty in every single moment. There is even beauty in the struggle, in the monotony, in the mundane. We often feel trapped by our first world possessions, like our mortgage or car, forgetting that to have access to these is a source of beauty alone. If searched for, beauty can be found everywhere that life is. There is beauty to be found in seeing one's position in life; in the very opportunity of reading this book. Beauty is not only related to pleasure and joy, but can be found in suffering as well.

Buddhist philosophy describes any negative emotion as an "afflictive emotion". It tells us that these harmful fluctuations of the mind are part of the human condition. By recognizing that afflictive emotions are valid and do exist, we can develop a sense of peace and happiness in this simple truth.

Putting these two assumptions together—happiness is the appreciation of beauty and beauty can be found in every moment—gets you to the logical conclusion:

Happiness is appreciating beauty in every moment

This is a rather profound realization, because if we are to constantly search for the beauty in every moment, we are sure to find it regularly; when we find beauty regularly, we live a happy life. More importantly, this is the foundation for a practical guide to living.

What is brilliant about this definition is that it moves

happiness from being a vague pursuit, to an outlook. It is not having the object that brings happiness, neither the moment, but the process of finding beauty (appreciation) that brings happiness. It can be practiced on any object, found in any moment. The source of happiness shifts from the object or idea, to the outlook of appreciating it. It moves from the external to the internal; from something that can be taken away by circumstance, to something that only you possess the power to take away. While subtle, this difference is paramount in that it moves happiness to be the sole responsibility of your mind, and leaves nothing to fortune or fate.

This makes happiness something that is not purchased or discovered, not found or lost. It is a thing that is practiced one day at a time. It is a choice that we have to make, a way of living each and every day.

Chapter 2

An Ocean of Happiness

Typically when we think of happiness, there is an analogy that gets thrown around. People say, "Happiness is like a wave." Some people are more turbulent and have big highs and deep lows, while others are more steady, with less turbulence but also smaller highs. The idea here is that there is a wave intersecting a line. Anything above the line is happiness while anything below the line is sadness. We'll call this the *happiness continuum*.

happiness

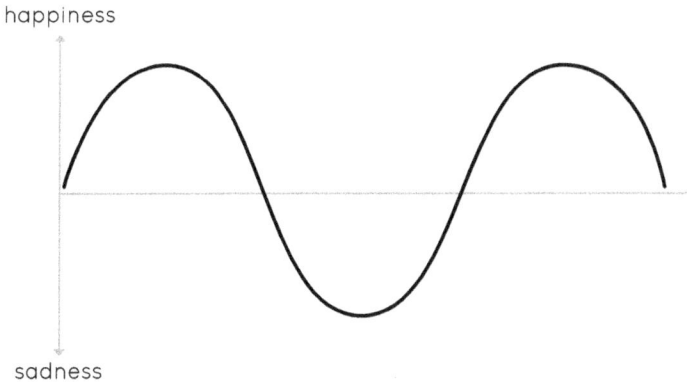

sadness

Without examining this deeper, it seems to make sense. Throughout life we have happy times and sad times, but this also implies that ultimate happiness is very unlikely and would consist of no pain and simply "good times". When aiming to reach happiness we often confuse pleasure and happiness.

If pleasure was the same as happiness then this would imply that people who spend most of their lives in pleasure would be the happiest. Ergo, the sensualist, the junkie, the selfish egoist would all be the happiest of human beings. We don't have to investigate this any further to see this is not the case. We know of many wealthy people with the money to afford any pleasure in the world, but whose lives are plagued with loneliness, sadness, and unhappiness. So clearly, a life of simply "good times" is not happiness.

To understand the difference we need to define them more clearly.

Pleasure is the feeling of agreeable sensory inputs. Pleasure is dependent on the quality of the world around us. To increase our pleasure we need to improve our environment.

Happiness is the act of appreciating the beauty around us. It is dependent on our ability to find beauty in our life. To increase our happiness we must strengthen our ability to appreciate beauty in everyday life.

It comes down to a matter of focus. Although appreciation does often result in pleasure, appreciation is the focus rather than the pursuit of pleasure. Pleasure is quickly nullified by repetition and is the desire of our ego, concerned only with how something feels to the self. Appreciation is the pure act of recognizing the beauty that an entity (internal or external) holds. Pleasure requires constant external stimulus, while appreciation can be practiced through internal will. While seemingly semantic, the differentiation here is that when practicing appreciation we can find happiness with very little, whereas when we focus on a life of pleasure, we grow insatiable appetites that continually need more and more.

A further problem with this representation of happiness is

that a life without any suffering is impossible. This leads to the widespread idea that happiness is an unattainable state of being, a distant oasis that one must constantly march towards but never reach. In other words, an endless pursuit of happiness.

Rather than settling with this outlook, we can rethink the *happiness continuum* as a *pleasure continuum*, where the crests of the wave are pleasure instead of happiness, and the troughs of the wave are suffering. In this sense, pleasure encompasses any positive emotion, such as joy, wonder, excitement, etc. Suffering encompasses any negative emotion, such as anger, jealousy, hatred, anxiety, etc.

pleasure

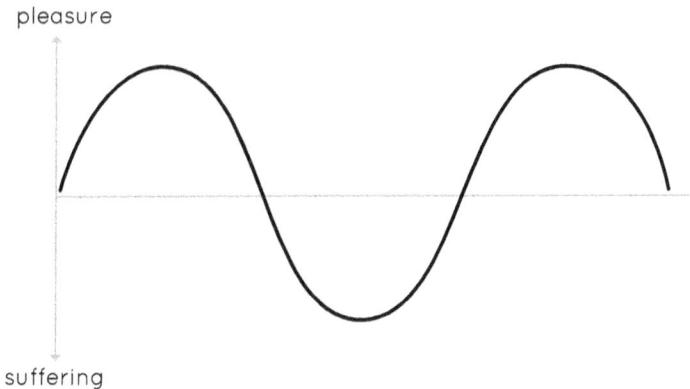

suffering

Already this wave more suitably reflects our fluctuating moments of pleasure and suffering rather than happiness. This may seem like a superficial difference, but we will see why it is important to remove happiness from the pleasure/suffering continuum shortly.

While this is already a more accurate depiction, we can go further by first coming to terms with the fact that pleasure and suffering are not absolute. We think of pleasure as everything above the baseline and suffering as everything below it. However, examining life we can see that our baseline for pleasure/suffering shifts with the environment and circumstance. For example, take a person in poverty whose pleasure/suffering baseline is at the level of meeting daily needs. We can then put this person into a modern first-world household and soon see their baseline will have adjusted to the environment around them. They will then require much more to stay above the baseline. What this indicates to us is that pleasure and suffering are relative, that our mind's perception of pleasure quickly adapts to the world around us. If we go on a rollercoaster ride once, we will experience an exhilarating ride with huge levels of excitement and joy; if we take the same rollercoaster ride ten thousand times, our mind will have adapted to the experience and find little pleasure in it. It would probably even become a monotonous experience of suffering. Similarly, this rule applies to the rollercoaster of life, we quickly adapt to the environment around us. As we spend more time above the line, reaching bigger and bigger highs, our mind becomes accustomed to these levels of happiness and our happiness baseline begins to shift. Things that once brought us major highs, now become mere quivers in our level of happiness.

This adaptation is known as the Hedonic Treadmill, the idea that our human minds are extremely adaptable. As our environment changes, so does our perception of happiness. It was coined in a study that compared the everyday happiness levels of paraplegics to lottery winners. It found that after a period of adjustment, the lottery winners were none the happier in life than the paraplegics. It compared happiness to walking on a treadmill, where one must continually walk forward to stay in the same position. In terms of hedonic (pleasure) happiness, this means that we constantly require more stimulus to keep our existing level of happiness.

pleasure

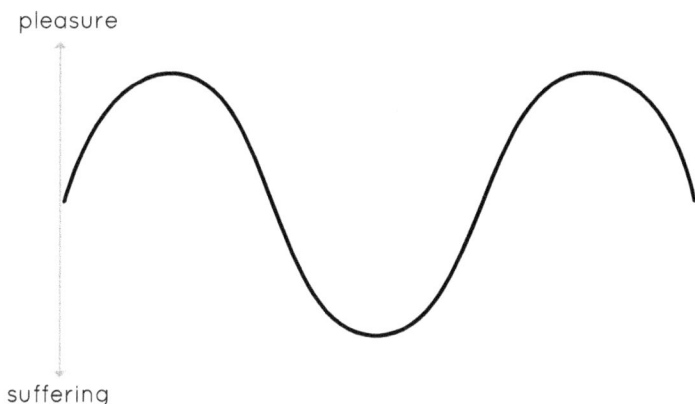

suffering

Looking back at our graph, we should first remove the baseline so as to accept that there is no absolute pleasure or absolute suffering; all is relative. We now have a more accurate depiction of pleasure and suffering, but how does this relate to happiness?

Matthieu Ricard, a biochemist turned Buddhist monk, can shed some light on this topic. In a talk on happiness Ricard described a Buddhist view on happiness: "Changing joys and sorrows are like the surface of the ocean, sometimes beautiful and quiet, sometimes shaken by waves and storms. Genuine, lasting happiness is like the depth of the ocean."

If we were to measure the depth of the ocean would we constantly remeasure it each time a wave comes and goes? No, because the height of the wave is insignificant to the depth of the ocean. Likewise, happiness is the depth of the ocean, and the turbulence on top (pleasure and suffering) is insignificant to it. It is only when there is very little happiness (on the shores) that the rise and fall of the waves makes any difference. Even the largest waves, when deep at sea, make little difference to the calm body of peace below.

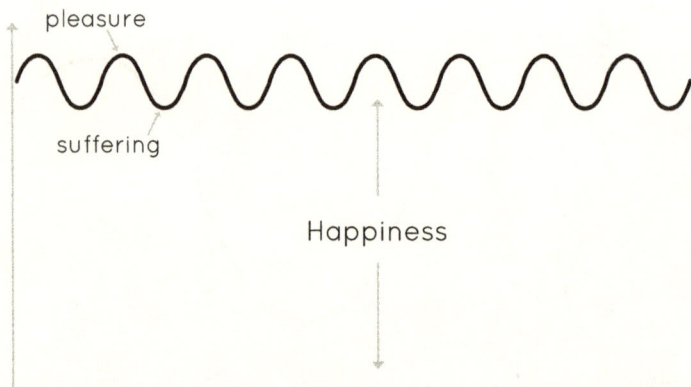

Using this idea, we can reimagine our pleasure/suffering continuum to look like the diagram of the ocean. At the bottom, we have a great depth of happiness that is undisturbed by the small fluctuating waves above. Some people will have larger, more turbulent waves, and others smaller and less fluctuating, however, both will have a deep reservoir of happiness below. The purpose of this book then becomes answering the question of, "How do we tap into this reservoir? How do we discover our ocean of happiness?"

Often without realizing it, we have spent our whole lives bopping on the surface of the ocean, getting thrown this way and that by the rise and fall of our emotional waves. This constant battle with the waves takes a heavy toll on us. We pray for fine weather, for a brief respite from this hectic existence, but even when the weather is clear and calm, allowing us some respite, it is only temporary. The next day, or the day after, will bring more tossing about. What we fail to see is that if we were to only swim down past the waves into the calm ocean depth then we would find the lasting peace that we so deeply yearn—freedom from the endless to and fro of the waves above. This freedom that we search for can be found only by looking within. It is not a reflection of our environment, as the waves of life are endless, but a reflection of our inner state of mind.

If happiness is the undisturbed depth of the ocean that rests quietly below the raging waves, then there should be nothing inherently good or bad in our fluctuating emotions. We should be able to be a turbulent person or a calm one, and neither would affect the deep reservoir of happiness below. Theoretically this seems true, however, in practice a turbulent mind presents many challenges to living happiness. When our emotions are very strong, be it pleasure or suffering, they have the tendency to cloud our mind. Take for example when someone is extremely angry about something. They feel the rage boiling within them. It grips their whole body so strongly that they become the rage. Their perception of reality then becomes extremely tainted; they tend to view everything through the eyes of their anger, hence, everything becomes more violent and harmful in their eyes. This is not an accurate perception of reality as it is tainted by strong emotions. The decisions made in this state of mind are not going to be the best. This is not just true for negative emotions but also positive ones. When we are extremely excited or infatuated, we often make decisions that are not based on true reality, but rather a rosy, romanticized version of what we perceive. This perception bias can then have a negative result on our lives.

This is not to say that we must all become enlightened gurus who have mastered their internal ocean to become a blissfully smooth pond. The real objective is to separate our fluctuating emotions from our happiness. The Buddhists call this state "detachment" and the Ancient Stoics call it "equanimity". It is not that we must try to stifle the rise and fall of the waves, but rather understand the irrelevance of pleasure/suffering on the depth of happiness. Achieving this in turn causes the pleasure/suffering continuum to fluctuate less violently and become calmer, in tune with the deep mass below it.

At the risk of sounding detached from real life, I reiterate: this is not to dictate that one must abstain from pleasure at all costs, rather, to understand that pleasure is irrelevant to happiness and that there are risks involved in admiring pleasure. When we build our happiness on the insatiable foundations of pleasure, our desire outgrows our satisfaction, bringing about more suffering. This path of pleasure is one that quickly leads to suffering and unhappiness.

Chapter 3

What is Suffering?

At the heart of Buddhism was a simple man named Siddhartha. His journey was one of self-discovery and enlightenment. It was through seeing the sources of suffering in the world that he became the enlightened one, the Buddha.

At the core of his teachings were these four simple ideas: every human life experiences suffering, the sources of suffering can be found, when we remove these causes we can eliminate suffering, and finally, the way to this lies in a simple eightfold path. One of the core roots that the Buddha identified was *desire*. While we don't have to convert to Buddhism, understanding how our desires lead to suffering, and prevent our happiness, is a valuable lesson that we can take away.

There are two parts to Buddhism: the Philosophy and the Religion. Many secular individuals choose to learn from Buddhism the Philosophy without feeling the need to practice it as a religion.

To understand why desire is said to be the root of suffering, we can consider a simple situation.

Imagine there are two men, each holding a gold coin. Both men are wealthy and have no real need for the coin, however, the first man loves money and hence wants to keep as much money as possible, while the second man is slightly more wise in that he knows the value of money, but since he is now wealthy beyond his need does not feel the need to hoard or collect it. If we were to take away the coin from each man, we can imagine the first would become distraught with suffering while the second would be indifferent. We have "hurt" each man equally, yet one will obviously suffer more than the other. This highlights that it is not the physical event of losing money that hurts either man, rather the mental outlook on the event. It is not reality that hurts us, but the *desire* for reality to be other than it is, that causes us mental anguish. When deeply understood, this idea is quite extraordinary. To think that with each event in life in which we have been hurt, whether it be a lover that rejected us, or a failed business opportunity, it was never the event itself that caused us any harm but rather our internal desire for this event to happen differently that causes us to suffer. Ancient Greek philosopher Epictetus put it best when he said: *"People are not disturbed by things, but by the view they take of them."* Like *happiness*, suffering is an outlook on life. It is the feeling of wishing something to be other than it is.

Suffering is the internal anguish that arises from desiring an alternate reality

Excluding physical harm, most of our suffering is self-inflicted. This is not to say that we should never suffer, that would be unrealistic. Life is a rollercoaster with ups and downs, and suffering is a vital part of life helping us understand the needs and wants of our subconscious mind. There are events in life such as the death of a loved one that we understandably wish had not occurred and hence rightly suffer from. However, on a day to day basis much of our suffering could be reduced if not eradicated by understanding the self-inflicting nature of suffering.

If we are to be realists about it, much of the suffering that we inflict upon ourselves is not necessary. Suffering is only useful in its ability to motivate our actions towards creating a different reality. If we continue to dwell in our suffering, we miss the positive influence that it can bring to our lives and exaggerate the negative. Moreso, since suffering is based on our desires, it is at the whims of our fickle and flighty mind. Our opinions that we hold about the world are always subject to change, hence we could be suffering terribly today over an outlook that may change tomorrow.

There is a story of a man who was building his dream home. He spent years saving, planning, then building a house that met his every desire—it was the perfect house. Understandably he cherished this house which he spent much mental and physical effort to create. It brought him much happiness. One day after completing the house he was standing in front of it admiring its perfection when a passing stranger stopped to marvel at his creation and said:

"You've built a beautiful house my friend, if only the windows were slightly larger."

The stranger continued on, leaving the man standing alone in front of his house. He inspected the windows that until then he thought were perfectly sized, yet now due to the seed of doubt planted in his mind by the stranger, he questioned it. Were they indeed too small? He had spent days picking the right window size, yet now from where he stood they indeed appeared too small. Distraught with finding an issue with his perfect house the man could not rest until it was fixed. He didn't sleep for a whole week as he worked on enlarging the windows. However a week later, he had replaced the windows with larger ones and was now again standing in front of his pride and joy, admiring it in its restored state of perfection.

Standing there in blissful peace, another stranger passed by admiring the house and said:

"What a beautiful house you have built, if only the tiles were black not red."

The second stranger passed on his way, leaving the man in doubt again. How had he not thought of using black tiles rather than these red ones which defile its perfection? Once again he was distraught and could not sleep until every red tile was removed and replaced with its black counterpart.

The man had now not slept for two whole weeks and although the house was now back to its perfect state, he was exhausted from the toil and suffering which he had endured. So he retired indoors to rest in his new home. Upon sitting inside a short while, the sun beat down relentlessly on the black tiles and burst through the large windows, heating the house to a boil. Inside the man sat dripping with sweat, regretting the changes he made to his perfect house until he could bear it no longer, and tore down the house in a rage.

Our desires are fickle and flighty. They cause us unbearable suffering for one thing until we change our ways, only to surprise us with more suffering for the opposite. By accepting the transient nature of suffering we can find a balance between the way things are, and the way we wish them to be; a happy balance between improvement and contentment.

How Does Desire Prevent Happiness?

To understand how desire prevents happiness, let us imagine that we have a pie that represents our happiness. When we start off, we have a full pie of happiness—this is how we are born. When we desire something, we are taking a slice of our pie and gambling it on a future wish. That wish could be a new car, a promotion, a wife, or anything else, but what we are saying is that when this future reality is fulfilled, we will have even more happiness than we already have. So we gamble our slice of pie on an uncertain future in hopes of increasing our happiness, leaving us in the present moment with an incomplete pie. As we take turns in this game–one that seems to last a lifetime–we are living with an incomplete pie. With each turn, we gamble away a little more of our pie. It is even likely that without realizing it we have gambled all our pie away in hopes of winning big later, leaving us with absolutely no pie left—a state of living akin to depression that some don't make it out of. Now, let us fast forward to the future when we are hoping to reap the rewards of our gamble. There are many ways it can play out. We could win back two slices of pie, ever slightly replenishing our empty plate. Alternatively, we could win the gamble but realize that as time has gone by, the reward no longer suits our desire, so in wishing for something else, we return our winnings to the table on another gamble. Finally, there is the reality that we just don't win. That the happiness that we were hoping to find in a marriage or promotion doesn't exist. Without re-alizing we are losing our pie one slice at a time until there is nothing left but a plate of crumbs.

The irony is that if we refused to play the game all together and remained content with our original pie, we would have been guaranteed a full pie of happiness—the exact same outcome as the best case scenario from gambling. In fact it would be better, as we would enjoy a complete pie for the entirety of the game.

The crux of this theoretical game is that desire is trading some of today's happiness, for the uncertainty of tomorrows.

Is There a Balance?

Admittedly this example paints a picture that we should not have desire. You could argue that if we never desired anything mankind would still be sitting in the caves, grunting around a fire. It is the human ability to desire a better future that has driven our ingenuity and creativity. There is no denying this: all great achievements of mankind have come from desiring a reality that does not yet exist and collaborating through communication to manifest it into a reality. However, if looking at any great achievement solely through the lens of happiness, it is not so clear cut. When looking solely at happiness, how do we justify the thousands of lives lost building the Panama Canal, or the millions of lives destroyed in World Wars which were fought for a reality that did not exist?

Rather than choosing between one extreme or the other, can we learn from them both and live a life of balance, between happiness and progress? What does this balance look like?

In everyday living our desires range in intensity on a spectrum between *willing* and *craving*.

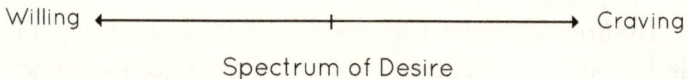

Willing ⟵─────────────┼─────────────⟶ Craving

Spectrum of Desire

At one end of the spectrum, desire takes the form of *willing*. This is the basis of what it means to be a conscious animal: having the ability to choose between two options, the ability to choose our desired reality. At this end of the spectrum desire is inevitable; to *will* is the building block of our existence. If we were to remove this from our life, we would become passive observers of reality, in a sense forfeiting our freedom. While desire at this level can be a source of suffering, it is not this desire that we are looking to reduce.

On the other extreme lies desire in the form of *craving*. Cravings are the desires that capture our whole mind and body making us feel an insatiable pull towards obtaining something. When craving, we are unable to concentrate or function on anything else; our whole being is desiring this one thing. This type of desire quickly corrodes our happiness by taking our current happiness and making it contingent on the fulfilment of this desire. In essence, we take some of our own happiness hostage, and only release it when the desire is fulfilled. This is what creates the motivation for us to fulfil the task that will end the craving. It is this happiness ransom that drives us to fulfil our cravings.

Craving is a "happiness ransom" that motivates us to fulfil our desires

This happiness ransom is the work of our "inner terrorist", a term coined by Christina Feldman, in *A Buddhist Path to Simplicity*. We have all felt the pain that terrorism inflicts on the modern world. It is a pain that we all wish could be ended, however we don't realize that we constantly inflict a similar suffering on ourselves in everyday life. By definition, terrorism is the manipulation of fear to disrupt and weaken a society. Inner-Terrorism is allowing negative thought patterns—such as insecurity, craving, and fear—to destabilize our minds, resulting in self-harm and suffering. To highlight the loss that craving brings with it, we can look at an old story.

There was once a boy who saw a beautiful apple tree while

wandering through the forest. The tree had hundreds of ripe juicy apples hanging from its branches. Amazed, the boy walked around the apple tree inspecting each apple when he saw one that caught his eye as the most beautiful of them all. It's color, shape and size was all to his liking. He wanted no apple other than his perfect one. Determined to have this apple he tried to climb the tree but the perfect apple was out of his reach. He sat down below the tree determined to wait for his apple to fall. He was so obsessed with having his perfect apple that as others fell around him he did not eat them, but remained sitting below, day and night watching his perfect apple in anticipation for it to drop. Time went on and countless apples dropped around him, slowly rotting on the forest floor. As Winter approached the boy was still sitting there, and his perfect apple remained high on its branch, the last one hanging on the now empty tree. Finally, one day when the boy was famished from hunger, a soft breeze swept through the forest and the apple dropped from its branch. By this time the apple had grown even larger and more beautiful, while the boy had grown hungrier than ever before. Catching the apple softly in his hands the boy was filled with joy and appreciation for his perfect apple. Wasting no time he brought the smooth skin up to his lips and sunk his teeth into the crisp flesh, only to find the apple rotting within and full of worms. Spitting out the apple the boy dropped it in disgust, letting it fall amongst the litter of other apples that had now rotted with time.

This story reminds us that our cravings often lead us astray. Worse still is that our cravings blind us to all the beautiful fruit that falls around us every day, moments that without being appreciated, decay on the forest floor of our lives. We forsake countless happy moments that are available to us right now for the chance of a single happy moment in the uncertain future.

The moral is not that we should refrain from desiring anything out of our reach. It is simply trying to highlight the spectrum of desire, the difference between willing and craving, so that we can find a balance between the two; a middle path that brings us maximum happiness while maintaining a necessary level of drive to take on the modern world. More so, when we do find ourselves using a strong desire to motivate us towards a goal, we should keep in mind that the true price that we pay for this is a ransom of our present-day happiness.

Part II

The Three Pillars

III

Although important, having an understanding of what happiness and suffering mean without a practical framework to live by will change nothing. It is comparable to having seeds for a flower but not planting them in fertile soil. If we wish to receive the fruits of our labor, we must give them a healthy environment to flourish and grow. When starting a garden we begin with the foundations, laying the soil. We too must start with a fertile environment for happiness to flourish. Before exploring the foundations, there is an ancient Zen story which serves as a great analogy.

The story goes that a man was riding his horse along a road when a passing traveller asked, "Where are you going?" To which the man on the horse replied, "I don't know, ask my horse."

This man, whose horse represents his emotions, is being carried through life wherever his fickle and flighty emotions choose. As you can imagine, if this man were trying to reach the next town, his journey would be very slow and arduous as his horse would be temperamental, stopping here and there, constantly changing directions as it saw fit.

For this man to reach the next town he must learn to master his horse. If he attempts to train his horse in a state of anger or frustration, he will fail to understand it properly. Hence, he first needs a *calm mind*. Next he must understand what the horse's motivations, fears and desires are. He would be unable to train the horse by offering it a piece of meat, horses don't like meat. This process of understanding our emotions is called *self-insight*, a way of looking within to understand the workings of our emotional mind. Mastery of his horse does not simply mean obedience; it is by understanding and listening to the horse that the rider will know when it is tired and needs rest, or when there is danger lurking that he cannot sense. Hence, he must not be a dictator over the horse but a leader who listens to and guides the horse. After training his horse, the man is now in full control over where he wants to go, however, without an understanding of how to navigate himself from one town to the next, he will be no better off than before. The final skill for the man is *external-insight*, the process of learning from the world around us and generating wisdom.

The three pillars of happiness that we will look at are:

||| 1. Calm Mind
         2. Self-Insight
         3. External-Insight

Each can be cultivated separately with a simple daily habit. However ultimately, all three are interdependent on one another. For example, as we start developing a calm mind, we will need to cultivate self-insight to progress. Similarly, as we seek to develop external-insight, we will need a calm mind in order to see reality clearly. Sustainable happiness requires the active cultivation and application of all three aspects.

Similar to the ocean metaphor of happiness, this Zen story reminds us that we should not aim to silence our emotions, but listen to them in order to better understand them. This will enable us to make better decisions in life and not be ruled by their fickle nature.

In the following chapters we will discuss in detail the three foundations of happiness. In doing so we will exploring the internal workings of the mind. For simplicities sake, any internal thoughts, emotions, fears, insecurities, etc. will be referred to as **fluctuations** of the mind. Hence following, when we refer to "observing the fluctuations" or "understanding the fluctuations", we mean observing and understanding the thoughts, emotions, fears and insecurities of our mind.

Chapter 4

Calm Mind

III

Our brains have evolved over thousands of years of evolution. They are the governors of our day-to-day lives and have kept us alive and prospering as a species thus far. Despite this, happiness seems a task that they are ill suited for. This is because our minds are not wired for happiness, but for survival. Their purpose is to ensure survival, not enjoyment. They do this desiring *better*. While "better" keeps us alive, it does not always equate to happier. Better for a tiger, means a higher social standing in the pack, meaning an improved chance of finding a mate and passing on his unique strand of life. As humans living in the modern day with shelter, food and safety, we need to realize that we have fulfilled our primitive goal and reign back our overcharged minds, to bring about a balance between our primitive and conscious minds; a balance between *better* and *happiness*.

Before we can balance our mind, it needs to be calm. Trying to change a noisy mind is like trying to fix a boat in a raging storm. With each part of the boat that is fixed, another will be damaged in the same time. This patching of the boat will not last and needs to be fixed before it can sail strong again. To do this the captain must first find a way to calmer waters else all his attempts to fix the boat will be in vain. Our minds, like the storm, are extremely complex and hazardous. It is impossible to identify the root of our problems while our minds are racing. If we don't calm our mind when looking within, then a problem which appears to stem from one issue could really lie with another.

Having a calm mind allows us to see reality clearly; it allows us to strip back the patterns and assumptions we make about life and see the world as it really is. A calm mind allows us to make better, unbiased decisions in life; it prevents us from getting overly attached to the transient, petty aspects of life and focus on those which are truly important. When we spend time observing the workings of our mind, the thoughts and emotions that arise become familiar to us. This allows us to greet them warmly since we know their true origins. The goal is to allow them to rise without repression, but they need not stay. Deep understanding of our mind is the key to mastering it. Buddha taught that "the wise man finds great joy in a mind self-controlled". His teachings focus on not repressing emotions, but understanding and accepting them as part of the human condition. Only then can we free ourselves from the turbulent waves of pleasure and suffering. As our inner awareness increases, our inner calmness does too. A calm mind allows us to face any situation and see the immense beauty in it; to face any moment and find happiness in it. A calm mind that is free from the stresses of anxiety and craving will also be able to understand new concepts much deeper. Take for example the idea that *happiness is finding beauty in every moment*. Hearing this is one thing, contemplating it through meditation is another, and living it is the ultimate level of understanding. Only when something has been taken from an idea all the way through to an inner truth, can we say we really understand it.

Cultivating a Calm Mind

The process of calming, clearing and mastering the mind is called meditation; it has been around since the beginning of recorded time. Buddha taught that sitting quietly and observing the mind was key to understanding life. However, having its roots in spirituality has often tainted its perception as a Zenful act that only the spiritual "woo woo" do. From a realist's perspective, there is nothing spiritual about meditation in itself. It is quite simply the act of learning to sit still and understand the mind. While many do use meditation as a spiritual process, I think for its broader adoption, dissociating the two is important.

Meditation is just sitting still.

Meditation is the process of observing the mind, calming the mind, and contemplating knowledge. Like our three foundations for happiness, these three components of meditation depend upon each other.

When we practice meditation to calm the mind our goal is unbiased acceptance. We are aiming to observe all that is going on within and accept it as part of the human condition. We are aiming to become at peace with *what is* in order to be free from what we feel *should be*.

Our minds have had years of unrestrained control, festering in harmful thought patterns that grow strong with repetition. Hence when beginning to practice meditation it may seem extremely difficult, sitting there in silence as our minds continue to race; thoughts of work, family, desires and regrets take center stage. To quiet our fickle mind is a journey that takes time and regular attention. When starting out, we often sit there and actively try to silence the mind. This, however, will achieve nothing but a headache. We should sit and observe with a non-judging eye.

Many people have tried to meditate once or twice and claim it doesn't work for them, which is the equivalent of saying that I went the the gym once or twice, but was still unfit, so gave up. For one to truly say they have tried meditation, it must be done daily for thirty days. Only then can one claim it is not for them. Prior to that they simply haven't done it.

Meditation is the process of training the mind, and like any other exercise, it takes time and repetition to reap the benefits. Meditation is not a mythical thing. There is no magic or faith involved. It is the process of bringing peace to the mind, and observing all that dwells within. Meditation is not something that can work for some and not for others, just as with physical exercise. Exercise is the process of physical self-improvement; meditation is the process of mental self-improvement. Both provide a specific value when practiced regularly. Both require consistency and disciplined practice. Much like exercise, it is easier and more beneficial to do smaller amounts regularly than attempting large amounts sporadically.

Form the Habit

If there is one thing that you take from this book, let it be a few simple habits that are geared towards your happiness.

The habit that we want to cultivate is **15 minutes of meditation everyday.** By committing a time of day to calm your mind, you are committing to happiness. While this statement sounds naive, it is far from it. If I told you that by practicing soccer every day I can guarantee you will get better at it, you would say that is obvious. Likewise, all this suggests is that by dedicating time and effort towards fostering an environment for happiness, our happiness will improve.

Mornings are generally a better time to meditate as it helps prepare us for the day ahead, while also taking advantage of the clearer mind. Start with 15 minutes everyday and gradually increase the duration as you feel more comfortable. While we won't go into the practical details of how to meditate here, there is a chapter at the end of this book which outlines some introductory steps.

Use this daily time to focus on your breathing. Simply watch any thoughts that arise but try not to pass judgement on them; we are so accustomed to judging others that when we first sit silently, we immediately judge ourselves. To gain a calm mind we must learn to accept and appreciate ourselves as we currently are. Breathe in. Observe. Breathe out. Accept.

Chapter 5

Self-Insight

Growing up we face many situations and experiences that shape the person we have become today. The fears and insecurities as a child get etched into the fabric of our soul; our subconscious remembers what our conscious mind has long forgotten. Later in life when a similar situation arises, these fears gently tug on the strings of our subconscious mind, prompting us to respond in certain ways based on past behaviour. If we got mad as a child when we felt rejected by our parents, it is likely that we still get mad today when we feel rejected by our partner. These subtle, learned behaviours are stored deep within us, unknown to our conscious mind. Without us realizing it, they are responsible for a large part of how we act on a daily basis. This is ironic in that a lot of our behaviour as a mature, intelligent adult is unknowingly driven by the fears and insecurities that have been ingrained in us since childhood. Or more poignantly put, our adult lives are driven by our childhood fears.

Let's imagine a story to help illustrate these ideas. Picture a young girl, let's call her Rebeca. Rebeca loved her dad very much, she idealized him. However, her dad was not very good at showing his love to her. He was cold and distant, and when she made a mistake he didn't let her forget it. Whenever she achieved something new, she looked for her father's approval, but only found a look of indifference. She blamed herself for not doing better, for not winning his love. As a result she learned that love was something that had to be won yet never could be. Always striving towards this impossible standard, Rebeca rebelled against the father that she loved. Fast-forward twenty years and this little girl is not so little anymore. She has a corporate job and lives in her own small apartment. At meetings when she is required to show the work which she has been progressing on, she feels the same deep inadequacy. This feeling turns to bitter disappointment and she becomes argumentative with her colleagues, rejecting their ideas and suggestions in an attempt to safeguard herself against her father's disapproval.

This story, in one way or another, is the story of us all. We each have fears and insecurities from childhood that attach to the core of who we are, and we unintentionally hold onto these memories and fears because they form our sense of self. The path of self-insight is inspecting our daily actions and emotions. By following them down to the depths of our conscious mind we can identify their true origin. The first step is not to try "fix" ourselves, but to simply *understand*. See what lies deep beneath the surface, what insecurities are the antagonists behind our daily responses. This process is an investigation of the *self*. It is about looking within, using an unbiased eye and searching for the seams in the patchwork, memories and behaviours that have long been hiding away. Only when we have found the root causes can we work towards forgiving, healing and re-growing our sense of self.

Self-insight takes months, even years, of regular attention and focus. If this sounds too exhaustive, remember that our bad habits have taken much more time to become as strong as they are, and that time we spent without hesitation.

Cultivating Self-Insight

"Until you make the unconscious conscious, it will guide your life and you will call it fate."

This quote by early 1900s psychiatrist Carl Jung captures the essence of self-insight; observing our mind to understand the fluctuations that lie within, enabling us to make more informed decisions in life.

Self-insight could more generally be described as reflection. This is something that we all do on some level, however, by creating a dedicated framework for it we can maximize its effectiveness.

Reflective meditation is simply the act of incorporating self-reflection into your meditation session. This enables us to utilize the focus which has been gained by calming the mind, to better understand any issues that lie within. This issue could be the difficult relationship with a co-worker, which appears on the surface as a clash in personality types, but when reflecting deeper stems from a hidden sense of jealousy that one holds for the other. It could be the frustration with your partner that surfaces as micro-management of household chores, but really stems from a feeling of inadequacy. Being able to sit quietly and reflect on the origins of our daily emotions without bias or attachment becomes extremely advantageous. This doesn't prevent harmful emotions such as jealousy from arising, it simply enables us to better understand their true origins and prevent them from driving our actions. This skill is extremely valuable in our personal, romantic and professional life. We are all human and all subject to the same range of fears and insecurities. Meditation does not aim to magically fix these problems, rather, to help us become aware of them, so that we can better navigate the turmoil they throw us in.

Another effective tool for cultivating self-insight is writing. Writing by nature is cathartic because it forces our racing mind to slow down and think in a linear fashion. As we jot down our thoughts on paper, they are mirrored back to our mind, which in turn helps us find any discrepancies. By reading back our thoughts, we view them as an external entity, and hence assess them more rationally. We are better able to see the irrationality of our fears when they are coming from paper, rather than our own stream of consciousness. It is this micro-cycle of writing/reading that helps us think in deeper and more connected ways. More so, writing is cathartic because once we have written down a fear, it often becomes easier to detach ourselves from it. Detachment is something that is taught heavily in Buddhism and is often misunderstood. The goal of detachment is not to become indifferent to our problems, friends and life, but rather the opposite. By detaching ourselves from our fluctuations, we are accepting them as part of life but not letting them define our experience; we accept that we have fears, but realize that these fears are not us.

The beauty of using writing to cultivate self-insight is that it can be used in a variety of ways. We can use it as just mentioned to inspect, understand and detach ourselves from the painful fluctuations of our mind. Alternatively, it can be used in the form of journaling to help us reflect on our past behaviours, actions and motivations. Simply writing down *what* we did yesterday can help us identify *why* we did it. This helps us to discover hidden motivations behind our seemingly simple actions. In another form, writing down questions and answers on paper can be used as a probing device. Start with a seemingly high level question like "Why was I frustrated yesterday?" and with each answer, keep asking "Why?" until you get to the root cause. In this exercise there are no wrong answers. The whole purpose is to unlock certain answers that usually get suppressed in your mind.

Coming back to Rebeca, the young girl from our universal story. Through regularly cultivating self-insight she would be able to sit back and watch the fluctuations of her mind. Ideally over time she would be able to see how her childhood insecurities resurface at work without her awareness. She would be able to accept these fluctuations as part of the human experience but not allow them to drive her argumentative nature with her colleagues.

Form the Habit

As part of your morning routine, add either **5 minutes of reflective-meditation or reflective-writing**. Either form of reflection is most effective when the mind is calmest, hence, first calm your mind with meditation, then watch the fluctuations that arise. It could be the fear over your next promotion, or ongoing frustration with a colleague. Reflect on your actions from the past day, did you treat people poorly because of your own fears? Aim to observe the fluctuations from an outsider's perspective; allow them to rise without feeling ownership over them. Then, with an unbiased eye, aim to identify the root causes of these fluctuations. Once you have seen this clearly, aim to realize that this fear, this emotion, is not you. It does not define you. You do not have to take ownership of it. Slowly, as you realize the emptiness of this fluctuation, you will see it dissolve away, making way for another fluctuation. It is as if you are waiting at a train station. You watch as the trains come in, you investigate where they have come from, but then you let them move on. This is an everlasting process of growth: continually looking within to identify internal biases that influence our opinions and behaviours.

Chapter 6

External-Insight

III

At this point we have focused on first calming the mind, and then observing its fluctuations to arrive at an understanding of the root causes that lie within. However, it is here where we can often see the causes but not know what to do next; we lack the wisdom on how to address them. This is where external-insight comes in. External-insight is the process of gaining knowledge and transforming it into wisdom through contemplation. Knowledge itself is of very little use to us. A teacher can tell us that 2 + 2 is 4 but until we internalize the workings of additions, that truth has no value. Even if we are given truths to live by from religion or society, it is not until we have internalized them through contemplation and lived them that we can say we understand them. Wisdom is knowledge internalized. Without wisdom we cannot live a life of happiness as we will sway to and fro between differing ideas of happiness.

Returning to the journey of our young Rebeca, despite now being capable of actively watching and understand-ing the fluctuations of her mind, she still suffers from the core issues that are unresolved. Addressing this is the role of external-insight. There are countless books from wise men and women of the past who have documented a solution for nearly every aspect of the human condition. It could be the Stoic approach to equanimity, the Buddhist approach to end suffering, or the Christian approach to loving compassion. There is a philosophy of living to suit every person. All that is really required of us is committing the time and energy to uncovering it.

Cultivating External-Insight

Despite the advances in technology over the past decade, books still play a special role in our lives. Regardless of whether it is printed or zapped to your device electronically, the medium of the book has changed very little. Not only has the technology of the book held up over time, but the ideas written centuries ago still hold true today. The written word has a powerful effect on the mind which no other form of communication can compare with. Written words can touch upon the most subtle and delicate ideas within the mind. They have the power to not only communicate knowledge but also communicate the essence of another being better than anything else. When you look at this book, these words, each chosen with care and consideration, when combined together form a unique strand of consciousness, so uniquely complex as to resemble a strand of DNA. The words written in books capture the essence of the author, and hence enable us to learn from them as if we were conversing directly, or more poetically, it allows us to rekindle the souls of those who time itself has taken away.

While in saying this, I knowingly run the risk of sounding old fashioned or naive, but if happiness is truly your goal, then the path is simple: foster a love of knowledge for both the external (knowledge) and internal (self-insight). As we acquire more knowledge with a calm mind, we will be better able to understand this crazy existence and the *self* in which we perceive it through.

With a voracious appetite for knowledge, one can illuminate the illusions of modern day life, enabling us to be less attached to the ebb and flow of fortune and fate. The more one reads, the more one realizes all great minds of the past have seen many of the same truths of life, and are saying the same thing in different words. The more one reads, the deeper one's knowledge becomes on the most important matter of all: life. However, reading these truths alone doesn't solve the issue, we must internalize them through contemplation and experience.

Contemplation is the process of focusing our mind on a single thing. This could be an external concept that was learned through reading, or an internal realization that came from reflection. Contemplation increases our understanding of an idea by inspecting it rigorously from multiple angles; it is the process of testing our truths as the metalsmith tests for gold. If you examine something with a flighty mind, you will only get surface level observations. Whereas if you examine it with a calm and steady mind, the observations will be deep and profound. Hence, the best time to incorporate contemplation is during meditation after calming the mind.

There are two types of reading:
reading to escape life, and reading to confront it.

We want to build a strong habit of reading to confront life. A good book shouldn't just silence our woes, but help us understand them.

Form the Habit

Dedicate 15 minutes each morning to reading something philosophical. I use this word in the broadest sense. It could be a spiritual text that deals with good living, or a scientific book that suggests ideas to improve your life. Regardless of the book, dedicating this small amount of daily time will ensure that you stay focused on your goal of happiness. If you are looking for an intermediary between science and religion, then the philosophy of Buddhism is a perfect place to spend this time.

Additionally, allow a minimum of 5 minutes at the end of your meditation for contemplation. Spending this short period of time when your mind is calmest to contemplate the ideas that you have been reading, will maximise their benefit by converting the knowledge into wisdom. Think of the contemplation as steroids for your reading; it maximized the effectiveness of your reading time by viewing the idea from multiple angles.

Part III

The Four Acts

Thus far in our journey we have looked at understanding happiness and investigated the foundations that constitute a happy mind. However, we have not yet really unravelled how to practice it.

Looking at the major religions and philosophies we can identify four main areas that lead to happiness.

Buddhism, as mentioned earlier, is both a religion and a philosophy for living. At the core of Buddhism is the idea of **mindfulness**. Buddhist philosophy reminds us that many of our woes in life come from the world which we imagine rather than the one we live in. It suggests that in order to find happiness we must live mindfully.

Through our own definition of happiness (finding beauty in every moment) we know that **appreciation** must be one of the core acts.

Looking to the Ancient Stoics, they would tell us that "A wise man is content with his lot, whatever it may be, without wishing for what he has not." Hence, **contentment** being our third act of happiness.

Finally, regardless which religion you look towards, whether it be Christianity, Buddhism, Hinduism or the Islamic faith, they are all based on the foundation of love. Thus, our final act of happiness that we will explore is **love**.

Hence, the four acts of happiness that we will explore are:

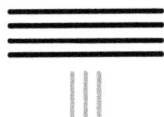

1. Mindfulness
2. Appreciation
3. Contentment
4. Love

Chapter 7

Mindfulness

We have all been around a newborn baby. Eyes wide open, taking in the vibrant sensory world for the first time. Imagine what that must be like, all of your senses overloaded with new information. You would see, hear, and feel everything, because nothing is normal to you yet. You have no concept of mundane because everything is being seen, heard or felt for the first time.

At this point, your mind doesn't know what patterns to look for so it processes every signal coming in. This is hardly scalable. Your brain wouldn't be able to continue in this manner, as manually processing the billions of incoming signals is inefficient. So our brains quickly learn to filter out the noise by scanning for patterns rather than processing individual signals. This signal matching is a trick our brain uses to process as little information as possible while still remaining alert to the potential dangers around us. It allows for past behaviour to be learned and associated with incoming patterns. This means that next time our brain receives the signal of, say, insecurity, it knows to use the learned behaviour of defensiveness to combat it.

However, the problem with this amazing feat of evolution is that as we get older, our brain gets better and better at looking for patterns rather than signals until we get to the point where everything is just a pattern. You drive down a pattern road, with your pattern gear shifting, sitting next to your pattern wife. You don't actually see the world around you as it is, but as the patterns that you have remembered it to be. Although this evolutionary skill has kept us alive by creating patterns of danger and safety, the problem is that we rarely step out of this mindframe. Every day we get onto the same train home, at the same time, probably in the same seat, and we ignore 90% of our sensory inputs, letting our mind unconsciously drift on things that are not actually happening in that moment.

Mindfulness is the process of dialling back the pattern matching machine and slowing down to see life more clearly. When being mindful of the present, you begin to see the world afresh. If you can break through the patterns, you start to realize that things actually look different than how you previously thought. Have you ever noticed when travelling how everything seems so beautiful? Each city is so rich with life, detail and texture; every day is filled with such potential, excitement and wonder. This is nothing more than your mind automatically resensitizing itself. The foreign location and break in routine has alerted your mind of the potential for danger, so it works in hyperdrive, no longer scanning for patterns but analyzing every signal that comes in. That is why when travelling, a single day of simply wandering about is so draining because your mind was actually active for the whole day.

The beauty is that every day of your life could feel as amazing as when on holiday, it's simply a matter of waking up to see and feel it. This change is more broadly called mindfulness, and it is simple to achieve.

Although becoming more and more widespread, the idea of mindfulness still remains under a veil of mystery. We hear about spiritual teachers preaching more mindful living and even companies teaching employees to be mindful. However, what is mindfulness? *Mindfulness is being aware of the present moment*. In essence, meditation is simply dedicated time for mindfulness. It is the act of sitting still and being aware of fluctuations in the mind. However mindfulness has its place outside of meditation too.

Practicing mindfulness throughout the day enables us to live life in a more conscious manner. This entails being present with the world around us, as well as our inner-world.

Being present to the external world enables us to enjoy life more fully. We are better able to take in and appreciate the beauty around us. Many times we are caught up in our internal worries that we don't actually see what is around us. Rather than seeing our partner, our eyes are blinded by our frustrations with work that play endlessly in our minds. Being mindful means awakening to the world as it exists. In this way, mindfulness is fundamental to living our definition of happiness. In order to appreciate the beauty around us in each moment, we first need to be aware that the moment is happening and that we are experiencing it. When we are mindful, time seems to slow down as we free ourselves from the internal monologue that plays endlessly in the theatre of our minds.

This leads us to internal mindfulness, which is the process of watching the fluctuations of our mind as they rise and fall. This helps us remain aware of any fears, desires, or insecurities that might be at play in a given situation. This awareness of our mind, enables us to make better decisions and react rationally. It allows us to see clearly our own jealousy, but not let it affect how we treat our colleagues. It is with mindfulness that we can apply the principles of self-insight throughout the day by watching our thoughts and emotions with an unbiased eye, enabling us to react with reason and logic. Mindful living is essentially a hyper fast feedback loop, where we are constantly watching our emotional reaction to the world, understanding the origins, then reacting in a positive way that is not biased by our own fears and insecurities.

When things are going well, it is easy to scoff at the idea that living presently can open us up to the unrealized beauty that surrounds us. However when things are going bad, we begin to realize how important and profound some of the simple joys of life truly are. Often, it is not until old age catches up with us that we realize the fruitlessness of chasing our insatiable desires, and realize the importance of the little things. We begin to find genuine beauty in things like family, silence, and nature. Ironically this shift in values often comes too late. We spend most of our lives chasing the intangible only to realize our error after life has passed us by. When people ask us what we are doing with our lives, there is an underlying assumption that anything we achieve with our life is more important than life itself, that the idea of simply living is no longer enough for us; one must live busily. Mindfulness helps us combat this by realizing that life only exists in the present moment, and that slowing down and becoming aware of this, is the only way to live a full life.

How to Practice Mindfulness

To simplify this task, we can break down mindfulness into two parts: first is inner-mindfulness, which means being aware of our own body, thoughts and emotions; second is outer-mindfulness, which means being aware of the world around us as it truly exists, free from biased interpretation.

Mindfulness is being aware of the present moment (inside and out)

For the first part, we covered much of this when understanding the benefits of a calm mind and self-insight. When we are aware of our body, thoughts, and emotions in the present moment, we are like the trained horserider who is master of both himself and his horse. We are then able to make better decisions in life by understanding where our reactions are stemming from.

By being present within our mind helps us be more present in the world around us. When we are living mindfully, we are aware of how our actions and words affect those around us, paying less attention to the voice inside our heads. When we do this, we can easily see how certain things we do and say might be hurting those around us. Although our actions may stem from good-will, if we are unaware of how they are affecting the people around us then our good intentions may be wasted. Hence, being present in the moment to other people's feelings and needs can help us be better human beings. Obviously, the goal is not that we never offend another person–this lies outside our control–but to be aware of when we do, so that we can try another approach, or understand how our well-intentioned actions are being perceived as offensive.

Life Hack* for Mindfulness
(*Life Hacks are a modern term for habit forming tricks that we can use to improve our quality of life.)

The problem with being mindful is that you first have to remember to be mindful. You can make yourself a goal, but as the day goes on and habits get in the way, you end up walking into your office at work without actually realizing how you got there. A trick for remembering to be mindful is creating triggers that you can use as a reminder. Personally, I found that lights in the dark of night has that effect for me. They make me stop what I'm doing and realize that I am alive. That this is life and it is not going to get any better. I might have more money later on, or more success, but life itself is never going to get any more real, more rich, than it is in each moment that I live it. Having lights as my trigger also serves as a litmus test to how mindful I am. On days when I am less mindful, I see my trigger as just a light and nothing more. This makes me realize that it hasn't yanked me out as much as usual, which prompts me to reflect on what is going on in my mind that is preventing me from living in the moment.

Find something in your life that can act as a trigger for yanking you out of autopilot and bringing you back to the present moment.

Chapter 8

Appreciation

Actively practicing mindfulness opens us up to the present moment, however, by itself, it does not ensure happiness. There was a young man who in search of happiness went to a monastery to train in meditation. After many days meditating he asked his master: "Master, the more I meditate the more aware I become... but this has only made me more aware of my misery."

If happiness is what we are searching for, mindfulness alone is not enough. Mindful living is the first step in the waltz of happiness. Once grounded in reality, we can come back to our definition of happiness—finding beauty in every moment. We can pull ourselves out of autopilot to live in the moment, and once there, we can more easily appreciate the beauty of life. We can appreciate our opportunities in life, relationships, even our own body. We can appreciate things as grand as a sunset or as subtle as our steady breathing. By utilizing mindfulnes we can appreciate things that usually go unseen in our hectic lives. We can come back to the moment and slow down our overcharged minds to tune in and appreciate the quiet strength of our heartbeat, the single most important aspect of our body that we take for granted every day.

Appreciation is fundamental to living a happy life because our focus is a precursor to the rest of our life. What we choose to focus on becomes what we think about. What we think about becomes what we feel. What we feel *is* our life experience. By choosing to focus on and appreciate the beauty in each moment, we are choosing what we feel; we are choosing happiness.

Appreciation vs Gratefulness

At this point, appreciation sounds a lot like gratefulness—an idea that most of us are already familiar with. Throughout our lives, when searching for happiness we have been told to be grateful for what we have, to remember there are others less fortunate than ourselves. We have been told to be thankful for the little things in life. If happiness was as easy as simply saying that you are grateful, then we wouldn't be here searching for a practical way to live it. The difficulty with this advice is that gratefulness is not always an easy thing to do. It is not simply a task that we can choose to carry out. Many times when given this advice, we genuinely try to be grateful. We tell ourselves that we *are grateful*, and that we *should* be happy. It is this "should" that undermines the effectiveness. Although we "should" be happy, we do not *feel* happy, which in turn makes us feel worse.

Gratefulness fails because it is not simply an action that can be performed, nor an emotion that can be felt. It is the description of something slightly more complex. It describes the feeling when appreciating something in relation to oneself. Sound confusing? That's because it is. To try and clarify this, we can imagine a sunset. If you tell your mind to appreciate the beauty in a sunset, your mind is aiming to (1) find the beautiful aspects of the sunset. In contrast, when you tell your mind to be grateful for the sunset, your mind is aiming to (1) find the beautiful aspects of the sunset, and (2) that you are fortunate to witness the sunset, because (3) other people don't get to watch the sunset. This is drastically more complex than the first. It is not only realizing the beauty that exists, but that you have the opportunity to witness it, and that many do not have this opportunity, and so therefore you are fortunate to have it, and hence, finally, that you should be happy. It is an attempt to appreciate the opportunity to appreciate. Mathematically speaking:

$$Gratefulness = Appreciation^2$$

The idea becomes grounded in metaphysics, (first realizing that you exist) then in sociology (realizing that your status in life is greater than others). What started as a simple way to reach happiness has become much more difficult in comparison to the simple act of appreciating beauty. Thus, although completely valid and useful, attempting to be grateful often fails to help people in difficult times. Whereas appreciation is an outlook that can be practiced by anyone with very little effort. Appreciation can be practiced on absolutely anything, even on itself. We can appreciate something as insignificant as a butterfly fluttering in the wind, to something as complex as a performance sports car; both can bring us a feeling of happiness.

When appreciation is paired with mindfulness, it allows us to turn a negative situation into a positive one. It enables the author who is bogged down with writer's block to realize that he is sitting with a cup of hot tea overlooking the beautiful Tokyo skyline. It is the mother who, frustrated with her child for breaking a plate, realizes that she has a happy, healthy child, and money to afford replacing a broken plate. It is the young professional who craves every day for a luxury car only to realize that his current car takes him everywhere he wants to go. Mindful appreciation is breaking free from the stories that we tell ourself and appreciating life as it is right now, not how we imagine it to be.

Life Hack for Appreciation

After developing mindfulness, appreciation enables us to turn average situations into great ones. After missing a bus to our disappointment, we can use appreciation to find beauty in our surroundings until the next bus arrives. We can turn bored frustration into happiness. All that is required is first catching yourself in one of these moments, then asking the question, "What is beautiful in this moment?" It could be the way the sun is reflecting off the autumn leaves. It could be the money you do have in your wallet for the bus. By searching for all the little things that are "right", you will quickly forget what is "wrong".

If you ever catch yourself wanting to answer, "Nothing!" Then you can have a laugh at yourself because that obviously reflects more on your state of mind than your environment.

Whenever you are mindful of the present, ask yourself, "What is beautiful in this moment?"

Chapter 9

Contentment

The modern era has brought about many changes. None however, have been as detrimental to human happiness than the shift in the combined morality of our society. Previously, social standards were set against two ideas: good and evil. Good and evil were the de facto yardstick that everything in our personal, social and economic lives were measured against. However, with the ever-increasing strength of capitalism, our morality has changed. We no longer worship these age-old traits. Instead, there is a new Goddess that we worship: the Goddess of Success.

We no longer think in terms of whether a company or person is good or evil, but if they are successful. This may seem obvious, but before capitalism this was not the case. Peoples value was measured based on their moral worth, rather than their financial. Financial success has rooted itself so deeply in our morality that when we see a massive corporation abusing the basic human rights of people, we might get angry, but there is nothing we can do because let's face it, they are successful.

As we have become more accustomed to the idea of success, we have degraded the value of contentment. When good and evil were the common modes of thought, contentment was not in direct opposition to either, it was in fact aligned with good. With the shift to a focus on success and failure, this changed. The idea of contentment has gained a weak connotation: to be content now insinuates an inability to be successful. Success–when used as a moral ideal–is the attainment of *better* and hence when used as a philosophy for living, is the insatiable dissatisfaction with one's current position. It is this constant striving for better, this dissatisfaction of what exists now and always imagining how happy we would be if life was better, that is the inner-terrorist behind much of today's depression, isolation and anxiety.

So let us try to restore contentment to its former undefiled meaning through the lens of happiness.

First, we must agree on a definition for what we mean by contentment. It is often used to describe the state of being happy. While this is true, it is also slightly more than this. We often hear the phrase, "Be content with what you have." This shows us that contentment is always in relation to something else. Without an alternative, or idea of *better*, the idea of contentment makes no sense; by definition it implies another option.

To take a logical approach to rediscovering the importance of contentment, and more importantly the inescapable conundrum of happiness when contentment is lacking, let us imagine an endless field. This field is all that exists in our imaginary universe and is virtually empty except a single house. This house is the only thing in our empty field and inside it there is a man living with his wife and three children. The house is beautiful. It has a small garden for his wife and room for the children to play. It is the embodiment of perfection in this imaginary world; it completely fulfils all the real needs of these beings. This man has no choice but to be happy. In his world (the empty field) he has everything and there is no idea yet of *better*. He, by mere lack of conceptual alternative, is content. His happiness is axiomatic, self-defined, irrefutable. He has everything that his physical needs require and he has no sense of better.

However, let us now place next to this house another house that is slightly better. It has a slightly better garden and more rooms for the children to play. The only thing that has changed in this world is that we have introduced an idea of better. But already we can see that the man, if he has no value for contentment, has a conundrum. He can no longer be happy with his house because he knows of one that is better. His happiness has been sabotaged, and he now desires the better house.

As benevolent dictators of this imaginary world, let us ease his pain and imagine that we give him the better house. So now there are only two houses in our endless field, the man and family live in the better one. Again the man is happy as there is nothing more in the field. He has no notion of better and hence has returned to being irrefutably happy. One can undoubtedly see where this is going. We add a third house to this field and again the man has the same problem. His happiness is destroyed as he desires the attainment of better.

In this scenario, it is obviously not the better house that makes one happy, but the state of mind; the ability to be content. When we abandon contentment and constantly desire better, it is impossible to be happy. One can follow this loop until the end of time, always justifying another desire that is slightly out of their current possession (better car, better house, better lifestyle).

This example is surely nothing new, it is more or less something we have heard many times in our life: "Be happy with what you have". The key thing to extract from this is that many of our desires are positional, in that they are measured by comparing what we have with the options around us.

Rich is not having a nice house; rich is having a nicer house than your neighbor.

While life does require financial stability and freedom of physical pain, it is important to scrutinize when we have reached this equilibrium, to recognise the difference between our needs and desires. We must learn the art of balancing *contentment* with *success*.

However, in a world where there will always be a better, how do we foster a mind of contentment? Luckily we have already defined this answer earlier: appreciation–finding beauty in every moment.

Rather than view an object, moment, or person through the lens of comparison, we should view the world around us through the lens of appreciation. If one can learn to master their mind and choose to find beauty around them, then one is *choosing* happiness.

How to Practice Contentment

A mindframe of contentment is one that we must regularly practice. We cannot simply say "From now on I shall be content and happy" as our mind is not yet practiced at this skill and hence, will likely fail. The key is to find things in your life with which you can actively practice contentment towards on a daily basis. One example of this could be food. Every day we choose a different meal to have, something new and exciting to bring us pleasure and joy. However, what we forget is that if a single dish full of flavors has the potential to bring us joy once, then in all honesty, that same dish has the flavors and potential to bring us joy an infinite number of times. The only barrier to this is our mind's inability to actively perform genuine contentment. So to practice this, choose a single (ideally nutritiously balanced) meal that can be eaten regularly. Start with a couple nights a week and increase over time to every weeknight. When eating this regular meal, slow down and appreciate the flavors it contains each and every time. Practice looking at your food and realizing that it exists right there in front of you. Through its existence, that also means that you exist. See that this meal you are eating does have many amazing flavors that as you slow down and appreciate, can be recognised and cherished. It provides your body with great energy; it is your source of life. If you can master contentment in one aspect of your life, it will then be easier to practice it in other areas: fashion, possessions, lifestyle, etc.

While this may sound lame and boring, that is just our fickle mind craving that which is new and exciting. If your main priority is happiness, and you cultivate a mindframe of contentment, you are travelling down a guaranteed path.

Life Hack for Contentment

Contentment is like a muscle. The more you use it, the better you get at it. Find an aspect of your daily life that you can simplify and practice contentment on. This could be food, fashion, possessions, or entertainment. Regardless what it is, each time you do this activity, practice slowing down and appreciating it. At first it will be easy, but as time goes on and mundanity sets it, it will take more and more contentment to appreciate the beauty.

Take one aspect of your daily life and simplify it. Repeat this every day, actively practicing contentment. Expand to more areas of life.

Chapter 10

Love

Love is a fundamental aspect of happiness, for our self and for humanity as a whole. In this modern age where ideas literally spread at the speed of light, we must remember that every action has a rippling effect. That our own happiness is intertwined with the happiness of all humanity. Hence we cannot look at happiness without looking at how it is perpetuated: love.

Before looking at how love relates to happiness, we must devise a rational definition of love to serve as the basis for our exploration.

Love is one of those topics that logic and rationality rarely dare to approach. We are happy to rule it off as an unexplainable, mystical occurrence that humans encounter, an idea above all ideas.

Without aiming to detract at all from the value and importance of love, investigating and understanding it from a rational viewpoint allows us to better prepare for the beautiful and frightening roller coaster that it takes us on.

Two great thinkers of the past that can help us on this journey are Plato, the Ancient Greek philosopher, and Immanuel Kant, the German father of modern philosophy.

First in *The Symposium*, Plato used the example of a flower to demonstrate that if we say, "I love this flower", it means we find it beautiful. More so, what we are really saying is that we perceive some "goodness" in it. When we say the flower is beautiful, it is because we think it reflects the ideal form of a flower, a "good" flower.

He went further to say that love is the desire to have that flower, now and in the future. What is interesting about this definition is that it highlights the craving side of love. That part of love is this burning desire within us to keep something forever, to possess it. This brings with it many interesting problems for relationships that we will explore later. Hence, what we can take from Plato is that love is the desire to keep something that we think is good:

Love is the desire to have good

This definition alone is not enough. Thus next we have Kant, who unintentionally gives a beautiful definition of love. Kant's argument comes in *Groundwork of a Metaphysics of Morals*, where he reestablishes the subjectivity of good– that an action with good intention cannot be assured to be good as the outcome may be unintentionally harmful to others. He finds one contradiction to this rule: the only thing that is good in-and-of itself is good-will. He defines good-will as the intention to do good; this can likewise be understood as love.

Love is the intention to do good

When we love someone, we have a strong desire deep down to do good by them. This is why we will do anything to help someone we truly love, because we are filled with good-will for that person. Unfortunately, there are times when we don't do good for the people we love. When the former part of our definition, our personal desires, overcome our good-will and hence, our actions become harmful to them.

Bringing these two definitions together defines love as both an intention and a desire–as something selfless and self-ish–that we feel towards things and people that we deem beautiful.

Love is the intention to do good, and the desire to have good

By simplifying love into these two components we can more easily explore how it relates to happiness, and ultimately how to love better.

How is love related to happiness?

We have all been the recipient of a much needed loving gesture. We know how much the little acts of loving kindness can greatly help us make it through a difficult time.

Love is the seed to happiness that can create much happiness around us. It is the *intention* component of love that when practiced in daily life leads to happiness, for others and ourself. When we have love for everyone around us, we are constantly looking for ways to help them achieve happiness. We look for things we can do to end their suffering and bring them happiness. By doing this we are gearing our actions and behaviour towards things that create beauty for them. This then creates a positive environment filled with things and actions that we ourselves can appreciate. Our appreciation then becomes our happiness. So by being a loving person, we have created a positive feedback loop that infinitely produces our own happiness. This is why *love* is a major factor to lasting happiness. By spreading love, we are planting the seeds for our own happiness.

Take a theoretical example of an empty room. This room has two people in it and nothing else. Let us imagine that these two people have nothing else in this room to find beautiful and they happen to think poorly of each other. So our two unlucky souls are stuck in an empty room with no happiness inside. Now let us imagine that one of them decides to do an act of kindness towards the other. This act of kindness starts in his mind as the intention to do good for the other (love). The other person who receives this loving gesture is likely to gain a small amount of happiness from it. The recipient then decides to replicate this good-will and does a similar expression of love, resulting in a little bit of happiness in the first person. Now, from an empty room with no happiness and only a little bit of good-will we have created a positive cycle of love that can result in happiness for both people.

"True happiness comes from having a sense of inner peace and contentment, which in turn must be achieved by cultivating altruism, love and compassion, and by eliminating anger, selfishness and greed."

– Dalai Lama

Living this life of love is often called altruism and is talked about as the key to happiness by many spiritual leaders. The reason altruism is said to be the key to happiness is this: Focus on yourself, viewing the world through your self-centered lens, and you will bear the weight of disappointment and suffering. Focus on the happiness of all by loving generously those around you and you will create your own joy through acts of love, leading to a happy life.

Further, learning to love generously can help us live happiness in another way. Our minds are fickle things when unrestrained that thrash about and inflict harm on themselves. They tell us stories, exaggerating a lump in the skin to painful death by cancer, a flirtatious comment to our spouse into a full blown love affair. The irony of these stories is that because our mind constructs them with such detail, we feel them as if they are real; we *are* dying of cancer, our spouse *is* having an affair. Without any of them being real, we have suffered them as if they were. These painful stories are the weapons of our inner terrorist. The steps to combating this inner terrorist are a calm mind, self-insight and most importantly love. It requires a certain amount of love to say that we no longer want to go on hurting our self, that this inner terrorism has to stop.

How to Practice Love

We all try to be good people. We try to love others while also balancing our own happiness. Given the opportunity, people are more good than bad. Often what prevents us from loving others is one of two things; either our personal desires conflict with theirs, or their actions don't seem to justify our loving kindness.

First is the art of balancing the two conflicting aspects of love: desire and intention. In any type of relationship, we often (rightfully) put our own priorities first, trying to ensure our own happiness. This logical reaction to the world has kept us alive and thriving as a species for thousands of years. However, this same rational decision to prioritize our own desires often leads us to much suffering. This happens when the balance between desire and good-will becomes unbalanced; when we focus solely on fulfilling our own desires and cravings, neglecting our social responsibility to love others. Unfortunately, no book can tell us exactly where this balance lies for every situation in life. This art of balancing our personal desires with good-will is something that we can only master with constant reflection and improvement.

Second is understanding the role that ignorance plays in motivating people's actions.

"All suffering is caused by ignorance. People inflict pain on others in the selfish pursuit of their own happiness. A truly compassionate attitude toward others does not change even if they behave negatively or hurt you."

– Dalai Lama XIV

Often when we are hurt by another person, our mind is overfilled with emotions of betrayal or frustration, preventing us from being able to see the situation as it really is. We are unable to see that the harmful actions other people stem from their own ignorance and suffering. Each of us have times when we are ignorant of something which causes us to harm others. Each of us have suffered to the point where we inflict suffering on others. Understanding this endless cycle of ignorance and suffering allows us to identify it and prevent it from being perpetuated by us. We can choose to end the cycle. This requires a compassionate outlook on others' suffering. Hence, we can choose to act with a loving response to the situation, preventing the cycle of ignorance and suffering from continuing.

By practicing love in this manner, we are able to create a more positive environment around us, which in turn will enable us to better live our own lives of happiness.

Life Hack for Love

We are all ignorant of something. We are all susceptible to wrongdoing. When we are struggling to be loving to someone we can remind ourselves that people's rude actions are a sign that they are suffering themselves. That the most common source of suffering is ignorance on one or both sides. Hence, when struggling to be loving to someone whose actions seem not to justify it, tell yourself:

"We all have the right to happiness. They are focused on their own right to happiness. I know that all suffering comes from ignorance and I am often ignorant too. So why should their ignorance dictate my actions? Why should I continue the cycle of suffering?"

Part IV

Practicing Happiness

The irony of how many people perceive happiness, is that it is often imagined as a destination; that once reached, the remainder of life is spent in a blissful state. In reality, happiness is an outlook, a lens through which we view life. Hence, this lens must always be at hand, and used to view the world. This also means we must continuously repair and polish this lens; it takes constant cultivation and effort to prevent ourselves from falling back into bad habits. Luckily, as we practice this outlook, it too becomes a stronger habit and takes less effort to maintain. In maintaining a mind of happiness there are several aspects to be weary of, several tricks of the mind that if misunderstood can wreak havoc to our best made plans for happiness. Or to return to our garden metaphor, certain bugs that if allowed to sneak into the newly laid soil, will corrupt anything that attempts to grow within.

Chapter 11

Relationships

*"The way to love anything
is to realize that it might be lost."*
– G. K. Chesterton

The West's obsession with finding a "true love" has corrupted our ability to live happiness. Marriage and domestic love have become such an important part of our lives, to the extent that when we are not in a relationship we are often down and depressed, waiting to find someone who can make us happy again.

However, this idea that we need someone to make us happy is very dangerous when looking to create a happy life. What ends up happening is that we place the enormous burden of fulfilling our happiness on our partner, and this burden becomes a prison that we build around them. The irony is that we are expecting a task from them that we ourselves are unable to fulfil, expecting them to satisfy our deepest personal desires that elude our own grasp. Then when our partner unsurprisingly fails, we begin questioning our love for them.

Early in the relationship, these expectations go unnoticed, as when first in love we find most of our fears and insecurities being alleviated by the freshness of love. For example, their loving reverence eases our fears of inadequacy, their tender affection soothes our bitter loneliness. In this initial stage, the love we receive from our partner masks our deeper anxieties, creating the illusion that they no longer exist in us. However, often as time goes on, infatuation fades, and the relationship dynamic changes. These insecurities start to surface again and we may find ourselves fighting with our partner over issues that really live inside. We often become dependent on our partner's ability to mend our broken wounds. We not only want their approval but *need* it. When they can no longer do this, we tend to place the blame on them rather than ourselves and become unhappy in the relationship. These difficulties in relationships have an obvious effect on our personal happiness, and what we often fail to see is how our own lack of personal happiness has caused the issues in the relationship. Like many things in life, we confuse cause and effect; thinking that our relationship has ruined our happiness, rather than seeing that our unhappiness has ruined our relationship.

Osho, an Indian mystic who has helped bring Eastern thought to the West, can guide us to finding happiness within a relationship.

"The capacity to be alone is the capacity to love. It may look paradoxical to you, but it is not. It is an existential truth: only those people who are capable of being alone are capable of love, of sharing, of going into the deepest core of the other person - without possessing the other, becoming dependant on the other or addicted to the other. They allow the other absolute freedom... their happiness cannot be taken by the other because it is not given by the other."
– Osho.

The argument that Osho is making is simple: before we can love another we must learn to love ourselves. He highlights that often in a relationship we expect our partner to heal our own internal suffering. This expectation is a form of bondage that will suffocate the relationship. We have all at one point in time felt the burden of fulfilling our own happiness. To have the additional weight of another person piled on top can make this unbearable. Osho claims that only once we have found our own happiness can we truly love our partner; it is only when we have mastered the ability to love ourselves that we will be much better suited to loving another as our love will be free from the guilt, possessiveness and expectations that often come with love.

From Osho's suggestion, we can say that the healthiest relationship would be two people who have found happiness separately, and then come together to share the resulting joy of living. Likewise, the most unhealthy relationship would be one where both people have struggled to find their own happiness, and hence expect the other to fulfil this task for them.

What we can take away from this is that if we wish to lighten the burden on our partner, we can look to find our own happiness externally from the relationship. From here we can bring much love to the relationship, while asking for little in return.

The "give-and-take" nature of relationships rings true to the definition of love we looked at earlier (love is the intention to do good, and the desire to have good.) Love is both selfish in our desire for the other and selfless in our intention to do good. This definition reminds us that we need to keep our relationships balanced and not let our selfish desires outweigh our good intentions.

Practical Takeaways for Relationships

1. First find happiness within, then share it with your partner

If we build our happiness to be contingent on our partner, then we are really imprisoning them with our burden. The healthiest of love is free from possessiveness and expectation. When we find happiness within ourselves, we are lifting the burden from our partners shoulders, lightening their load.

2. Love is polar in nature: it is a selfish desire and a selfless intention

Keeping the true nature of love in mind helps us be more mindful in our relationships. We can identify which of our actions are being motivated by desire, and which by selfless intention. Only by being mindful over these motivations can we better understand our relationships and improve them.

Chapter 12

Loneliness

"Once you have learned how to live alone, once you have learned how to enjoy your simple existence for no reason at all, then there is a possibility of solving the second, more complicated problem of two persons being together." – Osho

Our fickle minds constantly *underestimate* our ability to be happy in the present and *overestimate* our likelihood in the future. When single, we yearn for a soul-mate; when in a relationship, we yearn for freedom.

Often when we are single we focus so much on finding someone that we miss out on the amazing potential for growth the present holds. We fail to realize that being single is the easiest way to ensure a life of happiness. When you are single, you are fortunate enough to control all the factors of your environment; you are the only pilot in a small plane, free to choose where to fly. In a relationship, it becomes more complex. You are no longer the master of your destiny, there is another person who has their own goals and desires that get intertwined with your own. There is another pilot in the plane who has their own ideas on where to fly.

Alone, we often fail to take advantage of the opportunity that single life affords. We are so weighed down by the constant desire for a partner that we waste away the precious time that could be spent mastering our own individual happiness. Ironically, this mastery would help us in both gaining another partner, as well as bring more to the relationship.

While the loneliness of being single can feel like a curse, we would be better off to see it as a blessing. When we are the sole pilot of our lives we can spend our time as we see fit. We can read when we want to read, travel when we want to travel. This surplus of freedom is a precious gift we often don't realize until years later when we feel it to be lacking.

This isn't to say that this individual freedom is better than a relationship, it is simply remembering that when single, we should try not to spend the time desiring a relationship, but rather use it intentionally. Or to put it more poetically, don't spend the days of fine weather dreaming of the destination only to set sail in the storm; begin the journey to happiness when conditions are clearest.

Practical Takeaways for Loneliness

1. Take advantage of freedom to pursue true happiness

You will never have this much freedom to pursue your individual happiness. Instead of lamenting this time, spend it systematically learning and practicing a life of happiness so that when you reach the shores of a relationship you have a boat-full to give and ask for very little in return.

2. Relationships are not a prerequisite for happiness

All that is required for happiness can be found on an empty island. Don't delay happiness for a future where it "comes easier". Learn to practice happiness every day.

Chapter 13

Wealth

*"Wealth consists not in having great possessions,
but in having few wants."*

— Epictetus

When thinking about the question "How happy were you today?" or "How happy were you yesterday?", the amount of money you have in the bank rarely comes into the picture. We remember the nice dinner with family, the warm weather that brought a smile to our face, yet when we think about how happy we are *with our life*, we suddenly change our metric and view it through a material lens. We think about how respected we are in our career path, how much money we have in the bank, the car we drive, the house we don't own. When we think about the future, we overestimate the effect of wealth on our happiness. When we think about the present and past, we focus on how happy we actually felt.

Wealth is not a measure of money but of the mind

The importance of our outlook on happiness is extremely evident here. When measuring our life through the lens of success and wealth, we are usually underwhelmed and disappointed. When we view our life through the lens of everyday happiness, we are more often pleasantly surprised. All that is required from us is to remember that life is merely the accumulation of "yesterdays", that if we spend each moment appreciating the world around us, that is to say, spend each moment happy, then the net result of our life is happiness. Likewise, the more moments we spend measuring our life against some arbitrary benchmark of wealth, the more miserable our life will be.

The real problem with constructing happiness on wealth, is that it stems from a desire to be "rich". However, rich is not having a nice car, rich is having a nicer car than your neighbor. When you gain more wealth, you move into a nicer neighborhood, which in turn means wealthier neighbors, causing you to feel less rich. Rich is so relative that we can take a middle class man, place him in a developing country and all of a sudden he is rich. This is not an exaggeration, many people choose to do this. The change in relative wealth creates a real change in how wealthy they *feel*. That being said, moving countries to feel rich is hardly a solution that we can apply to our lives. More realistically we can reassess how important wealth is to our happiness. It is very common for us to build our image of self-worth on our financial wealth. This means that fluctuations in financial worth become fluctuations in our self-worth. As our bank account rises and falls, our feeling of worth changes too. What we often fail to realize is that financial wealth is not a reflection of our worth. We are all equal; all just animals on a gigantic spinning rock, waiting.

Through self-reflection we can aim to discover how much of our desire for wealth is for a better life, and how much is to sooth our egos.

Our finely-tuned capitalist societies are excellent at creating consumers. Unfortunately, they are less capable at creating happy people. The idea that wealth is better than happiness (or at least more realistic) is a vain and foolish idea perpetuated by the media and advertising the ones who benefit through making us insatiable consumers. This idea that we're all doomed for unhappiness leads to the idea that it is better to be rich-sad than poor-sad. While in some sense this is probably true, it is built on the fallacy that we can't just be happy instead.

"Money doesn't make you happy, but I would rather cry in an Aston Martin than a Toyota"
— Miserable Rich Person

We don't need to reject wealth. It is not inherently bad. If you can earn a lot of money in a way that you truly enjoy, that's great; money makes life easier and expands your possibilities. However, pivoting your whole life around the desire for wealth and expecting happiness to come along with it will only leave you feeling isolated and discontent.

Practical Takeaways for Wealth

1. Wealth is great, but happiness first

Don't slip into the day-to-day grind and forget what you are grinding for. Remember that happiness is the primary goal of life. Wealth can be helpful in creating a positive environment for happiness, but by no means is it mandatory.

2. Rich is having a nicer car than your neighbor

Our perception of rich is relative. Keeping this in mind allows us to gauge when we really have enough, or when we are continuously comparing ourselves to the next person up the ladder.

Chapter 14

Material Possessions

"The secret of happiness, you see, is not found in seeking more, but in developing the capacity to enjoy less."
— Socrates

We live in a time very different from any that has come before. Capitalism has proven to be effective as an economic model; people can get what they want, when they want it. Every craving and desire that we find brewing inside us can be fulfilled instantly at the click of a button, delivered to our door the next day. Never before in the history of mankind has there been this ability to "satisfy" our cravings so rapidly. Just one hundred years ago, not even the royalty had this power. This itself is remarkable; the average person living in a first-world country has more access to goods and information than the most elite ranking humans a century ago. In this age of instantaneous satisfaction, one would think that we are getting closer to fulfilling all our needs. Since we can have anything we want, we should be living in a utopia; individual happiness should be at an all time high with all suffering removed. Unfortunately we know this is not the case. But why not? Why, when we have the ability to satisfy nearly all our desires, are we still not happy?

Seneca seems to have an answer for us, *"It is not the man who has too little, but the man who craves more, that is poor."* It is not through fulfilling our cravings that we reach happiness, but by craving less. We spend most of our time in a cycle of craving, desiring possessions until we satisfy the craving. This exercise of fulfilling all our desires has an unwanted effect: instead of satisfying our internal cravings, it strengthens our ability to crave. The more we crave and satisfy ourselves, the stronger our desires become. This is why the material route to happiness is impossible, as each satisfaction raises the bar for the next. As we satisfy more, we desire more. Hence, our material desires tend to get larger and larger.

We think buying more stuff will make us happy, yet over time all we have acquired is a prison made of possessions that we must guard night and day. First it is our desire for possessions that enslave us, then it is our need to keep them that entraps us.

"Do not trouble yourself much to get new things, whether clothes or friends. Things do not change, we change. Sell your clothes and keep your thoughts."
– Henry David Thoreau

Two hundred years ago Thoreau saw the threat of capitalism to human happiness and urged people to reconnect with what is important in life–human life and nature. He was one of the many great thinkers who would now be called minimalists, people who live by the motto of "less is more". The minimalist lifestyle is becoming more popular in recent times due to many people realizing the negative effects that being a mindless consumer has on happiness. People are seeing that it is often the things they own, rather than what they lack, which is holding them back in life. That by reducing every part of life to that which is essential, we can free ourselves from the shackles of endless consumption. While we don't all have to become minimalists, the idea that "less is more" can be applied to all of our lives in one way or another, from the things we buy to how we spend our time. Through reduction, we can increase our capacity for happiness.

Practical Takeaways for Possessions

1. We need things to live, we don't need things to be happy

Buying new things is great! Everyone gets a rush with a new purchase. This is fine, but we must never kid ourselves into thinking it is happiness that we are buying.

2. Our possessions can become our cage

If we leave our material desires unchecked, then we run the risk of becoming mindless consumers whose insatiable appetites lie in the hands of advertisers.

3. The more you use it, the stronger it gets

The longer we stay in the crave-satisfy cycle, the stronger our desires for possessions become. To break the cycle we can simply reflect on our desires to identify if they stem from a real need, or a flighty want.

Chapter 15

Grass is Greener

"Be content with what you have; rejoice in the way things are. When you realize there is nothing lacking, the whole world belongs to you."

– Lao Tzu

There is an ancient story of a man who lived amongst the Green Hills. Every day he looked out to the Purple Hills that lay just on the horizon. The Purple Hills glowed with a magical sense of wonder, they seemed to be everything that the Green Hills were not. He knew life would be easier there, and that his happiness would flourish naturally. One day he packed up all his belongings and made the treacherous journey to the Purple Hills, only to find that when he arrived they were Green too. He looked back at his homeland and saw that it was the distance that made them appear purple.

This story is hardly anything new for us, we have heard it in one way or another countless times in life. Yet no matter how many times we hear "the grass is greener on the other side", we still go on dreaming about a future time when we will be happier. The new job that will bring us fulfilment, the loving wife who will nurture our happiness. We think that in this future world it will be easier to be happy, that our troubles will be eased and peace will be with us. However, we keep waiting for this future, and each time that it comes, somehow it is not quite as we imagined it, somehow our happiness escapes us again into the future. So this time we imagine the future slightly differently, again hoping that when it comes we will be happy.

"Putting things off is the biggest waste of life: it snatches away each day as it comes, and denies us the present by promising the future. You are arranging what lies in Fortune's control, and abandoning what lies in yours. The whole future lies in uncertainty: live immediately."
– Seneca

Seneca reminds us that the reality of life is this: we only ever live in the present moment. It is always easier to dream about the future and imagine life being better, however, the only way to happiness is living the future today. Life itself isn't going to get any "better"; you may have more friends, more money, more respect, but life itself will be the same. Your ability to be happy will always be the same. You will always have both times of joy and sadness, success and failure, love and rejection. Our ideals of a perfect life without suffering is impossible. Life *is* a rollercoaster. Only when we accept this and stop trying to conform our reality to an idyllic utopia can we learn to find true happiness in the present moment, in both the good and bad.

In *The Unbearable Lightness of Being* Milan Kundera gives a slightly different definition of the German word "kitsch". He describes it as the idealistic perfection, a world where the negative, violent, sad do not exist, where only happiness, joy, laughter can be found. At first "kitsch" sounds like something that only propaganda producing communist states are involved in, however each and every one of us falls subject to "kitsch" in our everyday lives. It is how we all imagine our future. We rarely imagine them realistically with ups and downs but rather as a utopia of perfection. We imagine the perfect husband who could never make us cry, the perfect house filled with love and laughter, the perfect family who are always kind and caring, the perfect wedding where nothing goes wrong. Kundera argues that this idealistic outlook is dangerous, that we will always be disappointed with what the future brings, as our ideals were rooted in fallacy. That our lives will never live up to our kitsch imagination, and more importantly never should! What we can take away from this is that by creating more realistic expectations of the future, we will be less disappointed when things inevitably go poorly at some time.

A school of thought in Ancient Greece was the Cynics who prescribed a healthy amount of pessimism in everyday life. They realized that we are often more hurt by our expectations of future events, than the events themselves. By imagining the future to turn out poorly, we will be better prepared for anything bad that comes our way. Similarly, any good events will be treated with pleasant surprise, and not be tainted by expectation.

Practical Takeaways for Grass is Greener Syndrome

1. Life is what you make it here and now
Stop staring at the Purple Hills. They are the same as the ones underneath your feet. Look down and enjoy the green grass.

2. Dream realistically
Life will always have a certain amount of pain and suffering, keeping this in mind will help you desire a more realistic future, one that won't leave you feeling disappointed when it arrives.

Chapter 16

Sense of Self

My work is not a reflection of my worth

One thing that often gets in the way of living happiness is our sense of self, and more specifically, how our sense of self gets intertwined with our self-worth. Whether in our private or professional lives, we often get offended by things that threaten our sense of self. We get offended when people question our ideas, actions, thoughts, opinions, not because we care about our opinions that dearly, but rather because when they are threatened, our self-worth is threatened. This is similar to what explains the mania behind sports. People who are "die-hard fans" of a sporting team take victories and losses extremely deeply. The only explanation for this is that they have invested a part of their worth in their favourite team. By rallying for their team, they are really rallying for themselves. When the team loses, they lose. When the team is victorious, they are victorious.

This defense of self worth comes out in more areas than just sports. All of us can recall a time at work when we have become hurt or threatened because our colleagues have questioned one of our suggestions, ideas or actions. This need to constantly defend "our" work actually presents a major limitation to growing as a person, and hence, living happiness. To combat this instinctive habit we can inspect where our sense of self really lies, and hence practice detaching our self-worth from things that are not truly us.

Growing up, we get a strong sense of *I* ingrained into our way of thinking and living. During our childhood, this sense of I (of self) gradually develops along the way. We learn that when we say "my bottle", this means that the bottle belongs to the self. When dealing with physical things it is easy to understand the divide between what is really I and what is not. Unfortunately, we do this with many other things, not just our physical possessions. We learn that these are my actions and hence that the actions not only belong to the I, but are the I.

Without realizing it, this leads us down a route of building our internal concept of I from many things that are not actually us. Our possessions, actions, speech, behaviour are all things that seem to define this sense of I. Because of this, we get very attached to these things. When our possessions get taken away or are threatened, we get so upset, not because we care deeply about our car or our house, but because without realizing it, the external object begins to define our internal self-image and hence it is the I that is being threatened. This is more clearly seen in our careers. If, for example, you are a painter and you produce a piece of art that gets rejected by its audience as "worthless", it is not the artwork as an individual entity that gets rejected but our sense of worth. Without realizing it, we are made to feel worthless because we built our concept of I on external things that are not really so. This happens on a smaller scale everywhere in life. The report you wrote for work or the dinner you made for your loved one. We constantly intertwine our sense of I with external things that are not *us*. We can look at some common areas where our sense of self is falsely attached.

We are not our possessions. We often buy things that make

us appear a certain way; we buy Nikes to look cool, a Mercedes to look classy. We think that by purchasing these items, we will inherit part of their character. While socially this holds true–we think people in a Mercedes are more classy than those in a Toyota–logically we know this is false. We know that the car you drive changes nothing about who you are as a person. So first one down: *We are not our possessions*.

Next is our actions, speech, and behaviour. These are the external reflections of our *will*. This is the most common basis for what we judge each other on. When one of these are questioned by someone, we immediately take offense because we feel that the worth of our behaviour is a reflection of our self-worth. What this outlook is forgetting is that we all make good and bad decisions. Our actions, speech and behaviour are reflections of the decisions we make. Yes, sometimes we make a "bad" decision. Does this mean that we are "bad"? Not at all. It means the decision we made was the wrong one. It means there is something for us to learn, something we are ignorant of which led us to make the wrong decision. By detaching our self worth from our behaviours it enables us to more critically assess them with an unbiased eye. This in turn enables us to learn from them much more than if we were to instinctively defend them. *We are not our behaviour*.

To give an example, when I'm not reading and writing, I work as a Software Designer. My work consists of designing the interface that you see when you interact with a piece of software. This means understanding how people think and interact with computers. I then have to translate that into a design that feels natural to the user. After creating a new design, I show them to team members. This is the point where my sense of self comes into play. I have spent hours creating these designs, and hence to me, they appear as a reflection of my worth. If these designs get rejected, then it is my worth as a Software Designer, or even as a human being, that is getting rejected. To combat this natural instinct, I tell myself one thing before presenting any design:

My work is not a reflection of my worth

This helps me detach my sense of self-worth from the quality of my work. Some days the designs are great, some days they are shit. The only way to produce the best work is for me to detach my self-worth from my work. It enables me to actively seek criticism on how to improve the designs without being deterred by the fear of people hurting my feelings in the process.

This outlook is partly inspired by Buddhist detachment–the technique of understanding, and then letting be, the fluctuations of life–but also from the deep introspection that we have covered above. We constantly misinterpret reality due to learned behaviour, social norms, etc. We build our sense of self on many things that are not really so. This opens us up to getting hurt and offended by other's views and opinions. When the value of these things come into question, we begin to question our value as human beings.

Detaching our self-worth allows us to be a better friend, lover, and person. We become less prone to offence and more understanding of others' opinions. More importantly we are able join others in investigating our actions with an unbiased eye, seeing the actions for what they are and not becoming attached to them because they are "our own".

Practical Takeaways for Sense of Self

1. Our possessions, actions, speech and behaviours do not define our self-worth

These are reflections of our choices, not of our self-worth. This outlook can help us be less defensive against criticism, and in turn grow to be better people.

2. "My ___ is not a reflection of my worth"

Say this to yourself when dealing with subjects that may lead to damaging your sense of self-worth. When deeply inspected our self-worth is intrinsic and untouchable.

Chapter 17

Failure

"Failures, repeated failures, are finger posts on the road to achievement. One fails forward toward success."

– C. S. Lewis

Humans are social animals. Success generally means moving up in the pack, and failure means moving down. This primal instinct generally gets tied up in our construct of happiness; we think that successful people are happy and people who fail are unhappy. We think that our failures are a reflection of our worth. That when we fail to succeed, not only have we failed, but we *are* a failure. Our sense of self gets tied up in our success and failures.

This mindset is so deeply instilled within us that we find it difficult to believe that a "loser" can be happy.

You may have heard the famous story of how Thomas Edison failed over 10,000 times before creating the first commercial light bulb. "I have not failed. I've just found 10,000 ways that won't work." Failure is inevitable in life. It is a fundamental component of how we learn. We can read a book on how to bake a cake, but only when we have tried, failed, then tried again, do we really know how to bake a cake. We need to know what mistakes to look out for, what adjustments we can make to the recipe, and all the other fundamentals of baking before we can consider ourselves proficient.

The same applies to all of life. If failure is such a critical part of the human experience, we need to change the relationship between failure and happiness. We need an outlook on failure that enables us to still be happy.

Part of that is accepting that failure is a part of life, part of the human condition. When we are able to accept that failure is as core a part of life as any other, then we are able to prevent the suffering that it often brings with it. We can look at failure as a humble teacher of life, helping us learn about the ourselves and the world. This outlook enables us to change failure from a thing of pain and suffering to something that we can respect. We can respect our past failures for teaching us important lessons. We can respect our future failures for teaching us what we do not yet know.

"Do not be embarrassed by your failures,
learn from them and start again."
– Richard Branson

Many successful modern day entrepreneurs share this mindset about failure. They view it as a learning tool. When they fail, they deconstruct the causes, learn as much from it as possible, then move on. They become a sponge, soaking up the lessons until they are full, then letting go of the failure by accepting it for what it is.

How do we then maintain our happiness, even while failing? Again, it comes down to our outlook. If we view the failure through the lens of learning rather than through the lens of "self-worth", we can see the failure for what it truly is: one of the thousands of lessons in life that grow us as a human being.

Practical Takeaways for Failing

1. Failure is our teacher in life

We can only say we have learnt when we know what works as well as what does not work. Each failure is one way that doesn't work.

2. Failure does not have to mean unhappiness

Remember that we all fail in life, it is a fundamental part of the human experience. Why should we let something so fundamental to the act of living prevent us from being happy?

Chapter 18

Drive (Motivation)

*"Every advancement in the history of mankind
has come from a loving heart."*

– said no one, ever.

We would be lying to ourselves to think that the modern world as we know it has been created solely out of love, compassion, and the desire to spread happiness. In honesty, most progress has been fueled by the insatiable desires of powerful men. Innovations in building, transportation and agriculture have generally been driven by ego and power. Even the space race between the USA and Russia that took man to the moon (our most over-glorified achievement) was driven by the desire for power, not peace. This is why since the boom of capitalism, innovation has skyrocketed. Although sounding cynical, this simply reflects the effectiveness of it as an economic model, as a motivator for mankind. Individual gains motivate us more effectively than altruistic ones.

At first glance there seems to be a conflict between happiness and progress. If we are happy people, content with what we have, how do we keep pushing the world forward? If we learn to be happy in our current environment, finding beauty in every moment, what is there to motivate us to achieve more? How do we find peace in our lives, while maintaining the drive to take on the modern world? How do we balance contentment against the desire for "better"?

A modern day man who has inspired thousands to improve their lives is Tony Robbins. If anyone understands motivation and drive, it's this man. He tells us: "In life you need either inspiration or desperation." That drive is usually fueled by either dissatisfaction or desire. The difficulty with this is that in both cases we undervalue the present and overvalue the future.

The only way to free ourselves from this conundrum seems to be to separate them. Make the present a place where happiness is found through appreciation and the future a place where improvement can be realized through constructive desire. Hence, the answer comes not by picking one or the other, but by choosing when to apply each. We can draw a distinct line between the present and the future. Happiness is measured in the present, in what exists here and now. It is the outlook that we live each and every day. Drive (desire for success) is completely unrelated to happiness. When imagining a "better" future in our minds, we can imagine one where life is easier–less stress, less financial difficulties, more freedom, more time–but not necessarily happier. While these are all things that impact our lives, they are not our happiness. Our happiness can be realized in each moment by appreciating the beauty around us. So our drive for the future is based on creating a "better" life, not a *happier* one.

> Draw a distinct line between the present and future. Happiness lives only in the now; drive is needed for a "better" future.

The purpose of creating this distinction is because desire

usually hampers our ability to be happy; it quickly escapes our control and destroys our ability to be content in the present. So instead we can take the desire aspect of success and use it as a tool for looking into the future, but not for measuring our happiness.

Historically, the motivation for success has been a very masculine-dominated arena that was typically driven by ego and the desire for power. This is what has motivated rulers to conquer new lands, cross unknown seas and travel to the moon. However, there is another insatiable desire that can be used as a more positive motivator: love. Oprah Winfrey is a woman who probably needs no introduction. What started as a talk show for stay-at-home mothers has grown into a billion dollar empire. She has shown that success, and the motivation needed to achieve it, can be driven from positive desires rather than destructive ones. Oprah's core motivation is the desire to help others. She has ignored the status quo for success and built her own guidelines for success, "Does this feel good? Will this help somebody?" Every decision she makes is driven by these questions. Contrast this to the typical motivator of many traditional businessmen: "Will this make money?" Oprah has shown that you can use a positive desire, such as love, to fuel your motivation for success.

Practical Takeaway for Drive

1. Happiness for the present, drive for the future
Never let your future ambitions taint your happiness. Measure your happiness in the present moment, and use drive only to create a "better" future.

2. Find positive motivators for success

Through self reflection, base your ideals of success on things that can be driven by positive motivators rather than selfish ones.

3. Mantra for happy success

"I will be happy in the present because happiness is an outlook on life that can be cultivated. However, when planning for the future I will strive to make it "better", not for the sake of my happiness, but because progress is a natural human function."

Chapter 19

Self-Confidence

"Superiority and inferiority complexes are both signs of a fragile ego. One of them is about delusions of grandeur, and the other delusions of insignificance."
- Caroline McHugh

Self-confidence is the output of our ego. When over-inflated, we feel empowered to follow our own path but also expect others should too. When under-inflated, we lack the strength to believe in our own path, hence follow the path that pleases others, away from our own happiness. In this sense, both superiority and inferiority complexes hamper our ability to live our definition of happiness.

So how do we find a middle way for our ego? In the words of Chade-Meng Tan–an ex-Google engineer who wrote the most practical approach to mindfulness ever, *Search Inside Yourself*–how do we feel "both as big as Mount Fuji and as small as a grain of sand" at the same time?

Remembering back to how we cultivated an environment for happiness, we can remember that it took three things, a calm mind, self-insight and external-insight. These same three things are the tools in which we can master our ego. Whether it be to steady the reigns on our raging ego, or muster some strength for our shy ego, it starts with calming our mind and then seeking to understand it. The greatest thing of all is that our ego is completely within our control. So if we are unsatisfied with the current balance of power it holds, then through reflection and understanding this can be shifted.

This process of understanding and nurturing our ego is the process of understanding our inner-self. As we strip away the expectations about who we "should" be and how we "should" act, we learn to be comfortable with who we already are. This inner peace is really what we are talking about when we talk about happiness. Tapping into the ocean of happiness is the key to living a courageous life. What this courageous life looks like is different for everyone. The inner self of Richard Branson is different from the inner self of Bill Gates which is different from the inner self of the Dalai Lama. The goal is not to try and emulate another person, but instead live courageously as the person you already are.

> *"You are already different, your job is*
> *to figure out how and to be MORE of that."*
> - Caroline McHugh

In a talk titled *The Art of Being You*, Caroline McHugh urges us to not only come to peace with our individuality, but more importantly, to cultivate it and learn to live it day-in day-out. By focusing less on who we think we should be, and more on who we already are, we can unlock the strength of our inner ego, using it to create positive change in our life.

The process of finding our individuality can only come through self-insight, by reflecting and observing the inner workings of our mind to find our true essence. Once we have that, it is our responsibility to live it boldly.

Practical Takeaways for Self-Confidence

1. Be as big as Mount Fuji, and as small as a grain of sand

Learn to master your inner ego and keep it at your service when required. Learn to be both as significant as the sun, yet as insignificant as a single ant; the world needs you but at the same time doesn't know you exist.

2. Be as much You as possible

With a calm mind and thorough self reflection, find the individuality that makes you unique. After finding it, strengthen it and live it boldly every day.

Chapter 20

Stillness (Idleness)

"Far from idleness being the root of all evil, it is rather the only true good."
– Soren Kierkegaard

This modern era has become one where people live to work. We grind away our days from 9-5 in hopes of living our lives on the weekend. Yet when those precious days do finally come, we cram them so full with socializing and leisure that by the end of them we feel more drained than when they started. So we take a holiday to recoup from our weekend but again spend the time trying to squeeze as much life out of every waking hour that when we return we feel as though we need a holiday to recoup from our holiday. You can see where this cycle is going. It almost seems paradoxical: we work to live but living seems more exhausting than working.

The issue lies in our cultural misunderstanding of leisure. Attempting to catch up on life we cram our weekends full of "leisure" not realizing that leisure is not the opposite of work–leisure is simply work without a need. *Idleness* is the true opposite to work.

Leisure is work without a need. Idleness is the true opposite to work.

Idleness is what recharges our batteries, giving us a renewed zest for life. Idleness is where we can learn about who we are as people and what life means to us. How many of us really schedule idleness into our lives? I'm talking about real idleness, not watching TV or socializing. I'm talking about the idleness that dances on the precipice of boredom.

The reality is that while in theory idleness sounds "nice", in reality it is often very uncomfortable. The image of relaxing on a beach soaking up the sun or sitting in a quiet forest is appealing to nearly everyone. However, when it comes down to it and we find ourselves with a moment of idleness that we were unable to fill, we often experience a brief period of enjoyment before the fear of boredom creeps upon us, destroying our serenity. So we pull out our mobile phone and scroll through a social feed. Maybe even share an ironic photo with our friends of how good it feels to be "relaxing" on the beach. So why is it that we love the idea of idleness but can't bare it in reality?

A rolling ball cannot be still

Our fickle minds are used to wandering to and fro wherever they please. Sitting down with nothing but our thoughts is frightening. Our fears and insecurities rise to the surface causing us mental anguish. As long as we are doing something, even just a menial task, our minds are prevented from wreaking havoc on themselves.

Given a choice between sitting alone in an empty room with only our thoughts, versus completing a simple mundane task for an hour, most of us would choose the task because boredom frightens us. However this is not really a hypothetical. We make this same choice thousands of times in our life. We tend to choose the task that probably doesn't need to be done, one which provides us very little satisfaction, because we don't want to be idle.

Moreso, our "Age of Success" has conditioned our fear of idleness. When we are idle, we feel unproductive. When we feel unproductive, we feel worthless. Nobody wants to feel worthless. Again it is our sense of self, tied up in the act of "doing nothing", that causes us the suffering of boredom. So in hopes of alleviating our suffering we do something. Not because we want to, but because it puts off the feeling of worthlessness. We occupy ourselves away from idleness, towards pointless productivity. So much so that you could argue this has become the goal of the modern era; pointless productivity. We measure a country's success by growing GDP (Gross Domestic Product), but have long forgotten what this growth reflected; an improvement in people's quality of life, an increase in happiness. Similarly we work tirelessly to be successful, but when we finally "make it" we realize we didn't know why we wanted to be successful in the first place. We thought it meant freedom, peace and happiness, but found it to mean increase in responsibility, work and stress.

> *"All of humanity's problems stem from man's inability to sit quietly in a room alone."*

Blaise Pascal, a 1600s French philosopher captured this perfectly in the above quote. Much of the suffering and anguish that exists in the world stems from man's inability to sit alone quietly. We would rather fight a war than sit in silence, rather make a living than enjoy living it. Apparently boredom is an innate human fear that we all share.

How can we combat this fear of idleness and make time in our lives to really recharge? Silent retreats are a concept that is gaining much popularity in recent years. Participants go to remote locations, usually in "exotic" destinations, where they spend 5-30 days in silence. No talking, no writing, no media, no mobiles. The idea is to resensitise your mind through extended periods of silence. By spending several days between idleness and meditation, people's ability to observe reality is awoken. By saying nothing, they learn to see more; by doing nothing, they learn appreciate more.

Every time I have told friends about ten-day silent retreats the reaction is always the same: "That sounds horrible!" For many of us, these silent retreats are frightening. The idea of idle silence for ten days is unbearable. The irony is that in a lifetime of roughly 30,000 days, we won't even spend 10 of them in silence. This fear that nearly all of us share is surprising. It tells us more about ourselves than any other question; it tells us that we are afraid of ourselves.

This might sound like an exaggeration, and whether you believe that boredom is the fear of our own mind, does not really matter. There is power in learning to be content in idleness. There is only one fact that we can be assured of in this uncertain life: we will spend our entire life alone inside our own mind. There is no escaping it. Hence, rather than distracting our mind, we can learn to be at peace with it. Rather than filling our lives with meaningless tasks that keep us busy, we can learn to find joy in idleness, giving us strength to face life when busy.

Incorporating Idleness into Life

There are a few ways we can incorporate idleness into our lives. First there is meditation, which we covered extensively earlier. Learning the art of stillness enables us to be better people when moving about. If we can come to peace with ourselves in the solitude of the mind, then we are less likely to let our fears and insecurities guide our actions throughout the day. Sitting still for 20 minutes a day is a small step forward in learning to be content in idleness. After practicing this regularly, you can begin to increase the duration of your meditation sessions. Alternatively, you can attempt longer sessions on days when you have more time such as weekends. This *will* be uncomfortable as you are pushing your limits but there is much that can be learnt from it.

Outside of meditation, another way that you can take advantage of idleness is when you next find yourself with a block of time that is unfilled and catch yourself reaching for your phone, music, or TV, stop yourself and simply sit there. Watch the suffering of boredom arise within. Fight the urge to check your phone or even tap your fingers. Just keep sitting there feeling the boredom for 10 minutes. Being comfortable with boredom is the first step towards understanding it. This exercise can teach us much about our own minds and hence is undoubtably a better use of time than watching TV commercials selling products you didn't know you wanted.

Practical Takeaways for Idleness

1. Don't put off idleness with meaningless tasks
Idleness is when our mind recharges. Learn to conquer your boredom and find peace in silence.

2. Dedicate regular time for idleness
Allocate time on weekends for recharging your mind through idleness. An hour gazing at the clouds with a cup of tea is time well spent.

Chapter 21

Ideas

Truth is opinion backed by vanity

As human beings, our minds have developed a trick to increase mental productivity when processing the outside world. What it does is group external phenomena into buckets that we know as *ideas*. The mental construct of an idea does not only define what something is, but also what something is not. This is extremely useful in processing the world around us as once we have bucketed it, our mind can use learned behaviours and actions towards it from prior experience.

However, there are two things to be wary of when taking advantage of this optimisation of the mind.

First, when we bucket things and people, it becomes harder for us to see the person as anything other than what the bucket describes. This causes us to oversimplify things and people. We begin to see them through an extremely narrow lens. For example, when we find ourselves hurt by another person's rude actions, we do not simply get hurt by their rudeness but mentally construct the idea of that person being built entirely of rudeness. However, in reality, this person may be rude but also may be going through personal issues of their own. They surely love someone in their life and are joyful to another. But because we have put them in the rude bucket and constructed the mental idea of them in our minds as being built on rudeness, we are unable to see all these other things.

Another example is when we define people by their beliefs. In our minds, we put someone in the Muslim bucket and build the mental image of that person as Muslim. We no longer treat this person as a whole, unique individual, but as a Muslim. The idea in which we have bucketed them to improve mental processing has become greater than the person themself. We are no longer able to see the complex and multifaceted aspects of this person because we are simply viewing them through one narrow lens.

The second issue with how our minds process the world through ideas is that they are often built on a misconception of reality. Our minds observe the world around us and translate sensory inputs into ideas which are then the basis for rational logic. When we misinterpret reality as being one way when in fact it is another, we run the risk of using false assumptions in our rational arguments, undermining their validity. For example, we have a strong sense of ownership over our possessions. When something happens to one of our possessions we get very upset because it belongs to us. However, when looking closely, the idea of ownership is built on a misconception of reality. Ownership is a social contract that we use in society to navigate complex interactions with other humans, but in reality, ownership does not exist. If all of mankind was to cease to exist except you, what would your ownership be with no others to respect it? So while ownership is extremely valuable and important in society, it does not truly exist. Our possessions are not ours, they are simply objects that others respect to not take away from us. However, while ownership may not be tangibly real, when we build our emotions on this misconception of ownership we can feel suffering that is very real.

So like the magician's assistant who sees clearly the method behind the magic but still plays his role, we too must respect the illusions that hold society together but always keep clear in mind the true nature of these ideas, never letting the idea cause us real suffering or playing the part too seriously.

Practical Takeaways

1. Avoid labeling people

Avoid using mental phrasing such as "He is" which leads to strict bucketing. Remember that we are all complex beings that cannot be simply put into one bucket or another.

2. Always question the obvious

While the person who we dislike may appear as "rude", can we search to see them as anything else? Are they also "considerate" or "passionate"?

Chapter 22

Stories

*"I am an old man and have known a great many trou-
bles, but most of them never happened."*

– Mark Twain

One day while on a three month trip to Japan I had a sudden onset of vertigo. It first occured during the middle of the
night when I woke to drink some water. As I sat up in bed the
world kept spinning. I tried to focus my eyes on the door but
despite my best effort, the room kept falling away from me.

The next morning things were no better. Any sudden
movement resulted in a seismic shift in my apparent world.
It was the first time when my senses which I relied on so
fundamentally had betrayed me. This had never happened
before, so obviously I was worried, I was frightened.

However, that wasn't the worst of it. A trip to the foreign
hospital proved to be frustrating due to the language barrier.
I tried to communicate what was happening to the doctors
through basic english and hand signing.

If the language barrier wasn't enough, I was stressed
about travel insurance. "Are they going to cover the costs?
Will they weasel their way out of it?"

The scans came back. I had brain cancer. It had already
spread throughout my body. I had months left to live. My
family was devastated. I spent the last few months of my life
traveling the world, coming back for my final days to be with

my family. I died at age 24...

Now, obviously none of this is true. It was all a story that I told myself. The vertigo went away after a day and was most likely just Benign Paroxysmal Positional Vertigo (BPPV) – a tiny dislodgement of debris in the ear. However, that didn't stop my brain from hashing out this story in the most intricate detail; it didn't stop my body from feeling those emotions of fear, loss, anxiety as if they were real.

We constantly tell ourselves stories about the future. Regardless if these stories come true, our bodies feel them as if they are. The story about dying of cancer wasn't real (luckily) but the fear that it generated was.

> *"The most terrible things in my life*
> *never actually happened."*
> – Oscar Wilde

Wilde is spot on. Most of our greatest losses and pains in life never actually materialize. We construct stories in our mind about how life might pan out. We physically respond to these stories with our emotions, but then life takes a completely different route and the imagined reality that we have already lamented over never actually comes about.

This process of imagining the future is a natural part of the human condition. It's how we anticipate and plan for the unknown. We construct in our head a model of the future world as we expect it to be, then we simulate how our actions could affect the situation. However, our minds often take this too far. We often continue telling ourselves these stories long after we have planned how we will respond. We unintentionally revel in the pain that these stories bring with them.

Catching ourselves in the midst of these stores is one thing, but then being able to bring a stop to them is another.

Humans have a weakness for endings. Have you ever tried to stop a movie halfway through? The suspense of how it ends will bug you day and night. This is the exact technique used by TV series writers to keep you hooked and waiting for the next episode. To bring an end to the suffering that these stories cause us we need to find a way of effectively stopping them.

"A young boy once asked his mother, 'What would you do if you imagined you were surrounded by a pack of hungry tigers with no one to save you?' His mother answered, 'I don't know. What would you do?' He answered, 'I'd stop pretending.'" – Christina Feldman

The key to preventing harm from these stories is preventing their repetition. These imaginations are not inherently bad. They help us identify issues that could arise in the future, and hence, prepare for them in advance. However, once these stories begin to loop, we no longer gain any benefit from them, instead we suffer unnecessary pain from them.

Using mindfulness we can identify when a story has progressed past the "useful" stage and begun to loop, inflicting unnecessary pain. At this point we know how the story ends. We know that our fickle mind will continue to do this unless we stop it. We can put our foot down and choose not to play it again, choose to think about something else and let that story fall away into the recess of our mind. Part of this includes coming to grips with the fact that the future will contain some suffering. It will also contain a lot of joy. Spending the time now lamenting what *might be*, will change nothing except wasting away the present moment which undoubtedly contains something that can be appreciated.

When we learn to stop these stories we can live much richer lives in the present and accept that "whatever will be, will be". This will give us more opportunity to appreciate the beauty that actually exists around us, rather than worrying about the suffering that may or may not be ahead.

Practical Takeaways

1. Stop the story from repeating

Stopping the story halfway through might be near impossible, however stopping it from repeating is much much easier. "I already know how this ends, I'm not watching it again".

2. Life will always contain some suffering

There is no trophy for predicting your own suffering, the only reward is that you bear the pain twice.

Chapter 23

In Closing

So here we are, at the close of our journey together, and the beginning of an even greater one: the ongoing living of happiness. Hopefully by reading this book we have laid down a handful of pieces in the grand puzzle of life. The rest of the puzzle still needs to be completed and the only way to finish it is through regular effort and focus. Don't wait for the next stumble in the dark to return to this path, but rather work on developing a love of wisdom, as was the case with the Greeks thousands of years ago. This will lead you back to some of the great minds who we have met with on our short journey here. Then, by diving into the depths of their pages, you can discover with greater clarity their profound ideas that served as stepping stones along the path of human thought, only to come back up for air, returning to the present moment to practice these ideas in the act of daily living.

"Happiness is a deep sense of flourishing that arises from an exceptionally healthy mind, an optimal state of being."
– Matthieu Ricard

In essence, what we have uncovered here is that there *is* a path to happiness. At its core, happiness is a healthy mind, which can be achieved by first calming it through meditation, then understanding the fluctuations that cause us suffering through *self-insight*, and finally by cultivating *external-insight* through reading and contemplation. These three foundations will create a healthy environment for happiness to flourish. Then with a solid foundation we can live happiness through the four acts: *mindfulness*, *appreciation*, *contentment* and *love*. In essence, remember that happiness is an outlook rather than a destination, we can live a happy life by finding beauty in every moment.

Here is a simple mantra that I use to embody the learnings from this book:

I know that everyone has the right to happiness.
Today I will practice my right to happiness,
By finding beauty in every moment.
And fulfil my obligation to spread happiness,
By being caring, considerate and loving.

The End

Thought Influencers

A bibliography of ideas

To reference the origin of every idea in this book is impossible. Even our most original ideas are influenced by those before us. So for this reason instead of a typical bibliography I have put together a more general list of books from people who have shaped my thinking, and hence, this book.

Buddhism

Buddhist thought has been a huge influencer in bringing together this philosophy of living. Nearly all of this book could be considered, in one way or another, a secular interpretation of Buddhism.

The Buddha

It will come as no surprise that the first, and most influential, Buddhist text was by the Buddha himself. *The Dhammapada* is a collection of sayings that the Buddha is believed to have said. After reading several translations, my favourite is the Penguin Classics edition, translated by Juan Mascaro. This little book captures the essence of Buddhist Philosophy in short, memorable sayings and maxims.

The Dalai Lama XIV

Possibly the most misunderstood man alive today. The Dalai Lama should really be thought of as a wise philosopher with a huge heart. While all his teachings are grounded in Buddhism, he by no means blatantly advocates it. My understanding of many, more complex Buddhist ideas such as "dependant arising"–the idea that everything comes from something else, and hence is everything else–came from reading the Dalai Lama's books. Personally, my two favourites are *Becoming Enlightened*, and *Stages of Meditation*.

Christina Feldman

A more modern Buddhist writer who captures many of the subtleties of Buddhism in a new and refreshing voice. Her book, *The Buddhist Path to Simplicity*, gave me a plethora of beautiful quotes and anecdotes to weave into this book.

Matthieu Ricard

In his TED Talk titled *The Habits of Happiness*, Matthieu briefly described happiness as an ocean–a deep mass with the turbulent waves of suffering above. This idea was the ember that sparked my rethinking of the pleasure/suffering continuum. After completing Living Happiness, I read Matthieu's book, *Happiness: A guide to developing life's most important skill*, which is a beautiful read, and highly recommended if you enjoyed this book.

Ancient Greek Philosophy

The birthplace of philosophy was over two thousand years ago in Ancient Greece. Socrates, the father of Philosophy, began by questioning the world, morality, ethics and reason. While he didn't put pen to paper, his disciples did. Much of how we think today is shaped by the thoughts of Socrates, Plato, and Aristotle. A few years later, a school of thought that is now known as Stoicism was born. While some of the early philosophers, like Plato, were more "academic", the Stoics were truly dedicated to the Art of Living.

Stoicism has been a huge influence on *Living Happiness*. The idea of contentment is deeply rooted in Stoic thought. Also the outlook of acceptance comes from the Stoics, despite sharing its roots with Buddhism.

Plato

If Socrates was the "father" of Philosophy, then Plato is the first son; a disciple who continued what Socrates began after he was sentenced to death. Reading Plato is great for getting a grasp on the fundamentals of Philosophy, for it is in these ancient dialogues that it was born. Reading his major work, *The Republic*, may be a bit heavy as an introduction, however, his smaller excerpts *The Allegory of the Cave*, and *The Symposium* are both insightful reads that were fundamental in shaping my understanding of many concepts; from love to how we perceive reality.

Seneca

It is said that reading allows us to converse with those who time itself has taken away. If that is true, then my conversations with Seneca are amongst my most prized experiences. A good introduction to Seneca and Stoic thought is his book, *On the Shortness of Life*, which is a small collection of letters that he sent to family and friends. Combine this with his complete *Letters from a Stoic*, and you have the best of Stoic thought in your hands.

Epictetus

When Buddhist talk about misconception of reality, I believe they are talking about the same things as Epictetus spoke of. His Stoic words in *The Enchiridion* serve as a small handbook for life that can be taken anywhere. While Epictetus was born a slave, he died a Stoic Saint.

Marcus Aurelius

Emperor of Rome, Marcus jotted down thoughts to himself on how to live and rule justly. His writings have been compiled into the infamous book, *Meditations*, and read by millions. In this he captures the Stoic essence through a range of circumstances that life threw at him.

Modern (Non-ancient) Philosophy

While the core ideas in *Living Happiness* are born from the combination of Buddhism and Stoic Philosophy, I feel it is impossible to disregard the influence of some more modern thinkers.

Albert Camus

Despite rejecting the title themselves, Camus and his contemporary Jean-Paul Sartre, were the two prominent thinkers behind the Existentialist movement. The core idea put forth in his collected essays (*Resistance, Rebellion and Death*) and novels (*The Plague, The Rebel*) is one of extreme acceptance; accepting life as we know it to be, without needing a higher power to find value in it. Directly, and indirectly, Camus has shaped my understanding of life and what it means to live a good one.

Jean-Paul Sartre

Existentialism is a word that many people misunderstand. There is a tendency for it to be interpreted as a kind of nihilism; a rejection of everything. Sartre confronted this misinterpretation in his essays *Existentialism is a Humanism* and complete work, *Being and Nothingness*. Like the Stoics, I see a connection between Sartre's acceptance of suffering and Buddhism. This connection made him an undeniable influence on *Living Happiness*.

Immanuel Kant

Considered the "father of modern philosophy", Kant had an extremely bright mind which he applied heavily to the theoretical side of Philosophy. His work, *Groundwork of the Metaphysic of Morals*, was pivotal in shaping my understanding of morality and love. Despite his brilliance, reading Kant will likely act as a hypnotic to anyone but the eager philosopher.

Death of Self-Help

A plea for recategorization

The categorization of self-help books is quietly killing our world. The fact that we only think to better ourselves in a time of need–when it is "help" we are seeking–breeds a selfish and isolated mindset which is behind much of today's world problems.

These books of self understanding and betterment should not be crammed into the back of stores, out of sight in the dark corner like some sort of shameful pornography. We should not be forced to scuttle into these sections, head low, steadily avoiding eye contact in fear of the stigma that being found out would bring. The idea that this aisle is for the weak and helpless who have already failed at living and hence need rehabilitation only perpetuates the lie that learning to live is easy, and that only failures need knowledge and guidance on the matter.

It is our *duty* as human beings in a global society to continuously better ourselves each and every day. Not purely for the happiness and quality of life that these books do bring (albeit a great reason in and of itself) but because it is the collective peace and happiness of our individual minds that, when combined, creates the peace and happiness of the world.

So please, let us abolish the "self-help" classification, and in its wake, reinstate a more appropriately named group of books: "Life" books. Life is the one thing that no matter your religious background, ethnicity or political standpoint, we must all learn to do, and do well. It was said by Seneca over two thousand years ago that "living is the only art that takes a lifetime to master". In our excessively materialistic world, we need the art of living more than ever. Not just in our low times of depression and crisis, but on a daily basis.

This is not a category for the old and dying; why should we start living only when our lives are coming to an end? We need to be constantly learning to improve throughout life.

Let our libraries and bookstores remove these shameful signs and rescue these books of knowledge and wisdom from their dimly lit corners of shame, not for the chance of profit but for the sake of morality; because it is the right thing to do. Each newly crowned shelf, center stage in our libraries and shops displaying proudly its plaque of honour that makes clear that learning to live is important, that this aisle isn't for the shameful failures but for the progressive new generation who constantly seek to master this age old Art of Living.

Creating a peaceful, happy planet is no easy task, but the easiest and most immediate step is by making peaceful and happy minds. That is why this change is not merely a matter of literary classification: it is wholly and truly a matter of world peace.

A Lesson in Sitting Still

A beginners guide to meditation.

Meditation is both nothing, in its cease from habit, and everything, in its awakening to the now.

Earlier when looking at the environment needed to cultivate happiness, we touched on the need to understand one's mind and emotions through meditation. While at its core, meditation is nothing more than sitting still, when first learning it can be confusing to know exactly how to start. For this, we'll briefly look at some techniques for those who want to try to bring clarity to their mind and life.

1. Location

The great thing about meditation is that you can do it anywhere; that old man you think is always sleeping on the bus, well he just might be a Zen master in disguise. While technically you can meditate in any environment, ideally you want a nice quiet place to keep your mind from being distracted. Especially when starting out, noise is one of the senses that seems to be accentuated as your mind is brought to quiet.

2. Time

When you start out, you most likely won't be comfortable meditating longer than ten minutes. It will be surprising how much focus doing nothing can take. Since you'll be doing this for the next thirty days–and you *are* going to be doing this for the next thirty days–you can start off with shorter lengths, and gradually extend the time each day. By the end of the thirty days, you should ideally be doing 20 minute sessions a day. If you feel comfortable enjoying the peace, then, by all means, sit longer, however, like any new activity, don't overextend yourself too quickly and tire of it.

3. Position

No, you don't have to have a meditation pillow, but since you will be sitting on the floor for an extended period of time, choose somewhere soft and your bum will thank you.

As for body posture, while there is no single correct way to sit, there is a generally advised position that has been chosen for its suitability to meditating. Sit with your legs crossed and arms relaxed in your lap. Overlap your fingers and touch your thumbs into a V shape. Straighten your back and tuck your chin in slightly; this will keep your head nicely balanced.

4. Eyes

Simply relax your eyelids and allow them to close 90% of the way so that they are open a slither. If you find that your eyelids are flickering that is ok, as you learn to listen to your body, you will realize how much stress you hold throughout it daily. They will serve as your peace-o-metre (the more stressed you are the more your eyes will flutter) but over time they will become still.

5. Breathing

Leave your jaw slightly open and rest your tongue against the roof of your mouth. Take deep long breaths in and out through your nose. Focusing your mind on the air rushing through your nose will help clear and focus your mind. A technique that works well for me is to imagine breathing in through the left and out through the right nostril, alternating as you go.

6. Mind

Now, with your eyes virtually closed and your breathing long and slow, comes the fun part: sit and watch whatever arises. Remember, the two core goals of meditation are understanding your mind and calming it. Imagine being a third party spectator to your mind; you are just sitting in, watching it as it thinks, desires and fears. Watch as thoughts and emotions pop into your head. Examine them, understand their roots of origin, then let them pass.

After watching the rise and fall of your thoughts, move on to simply calming and clearing your mind. Focus on your breath and find freedom from thought. If you try to block out your thoughts, you will achieve nothing but a headache. Instead, imagine your thoughts as if they were floating past on a river; as they come in, let them out.

7. Mantra

Some people use mantras in the same way as they use breathing, that is, to focus on something very simple and repetitive to stop their mind from jumping to other thoughts. You can use one of the popular ancient Hindu mantras or any short calming phrase of your own.

8. Repetition

As mentioned earlier, meditation is not the act of sitting still once, it is the repeated habit of listening and quieting your mind. If you truly want to master your mind and find happiness, then a commitment to ten minutes a day for a month is not much to ask.

9. Example

Following steps is always made clearer by a little story, so here is how a purely hypothetical session of meditation could play out. Purely hypothetical.

The Author, unpublished of course, sits on the carpet floor. He has been writing for six hours and his mind races with words and metaphors. Crossing his legs, he rests his palms in his lap, fingers overlapping and thumbs touching. Closing his eyes, he feels the weight of countless hours typing fall from his shoulders. As he breathes in, the dampness in his chest catches his mind's eye; slaving over the keyboard has its price. His eyebrows, stiff from the harsh computer glow, slowly relax and descend what seem a mile from their tightly scrunched position. Not even a minute in and he already feels better. He sits patiently and watches his mind. First comes a new metaphor for the cold winter night, being overstocked with pretty words in a notebook that don't pay rent, he lets it slip back into the night from where it came. Next comes something less romantic, something that lurks up from the depths, a vague unsettling feeling. Finding it difficult to place a finger on it, he watches it rise, questioning what it could be? Is it dissatisfaction with his book? No, he has crafted a work of genius, no author ever thinks lowly of their work. What then? Ahh of course, the antithesis of the former, the fear that such a work will go unread, that the value of him, the Author, lies in the value of his published work. Luckily the Author has read a thing or two on this very matter; he questions himself as to whether the book constitutes his sense of self? How could it? He is not an Author, but a Human who authors books. The worth of his book, or lack thereof, means nothing to the worth of his being. The book will be what it is, and the Author a valid human nonetheless. The vagueness dissipates immediately, leaving in its place a clear sense of freedom. Focusing on that freedom, he spends the rest of his time rejoicing in its solitude.

Thanks for getting this far.

The world we live in can only be as good as our collective minds. I believe the philosophy put forth in these pages can help make us all a little happier, and in turn, make the world a happier place.

If you share this vision:

1. Share *Living Happiness* with a friend (or ten)
2. Leave a review on GoodReads or Amazon
3. Subscribe to my newsletter at sebastiankade.com